# Company's Coming®

# 30-Minute Rookie Cook

*Jean Paré*

**www.companyscoming.com**
visit our website

## Back Cover

1. Hoisin Pork Stir-Fry, page 130
2. Balsamic Pork Chops, page 128
3. Orange Pork Sitr-Fry, page 129

Props courtesy of:  The Dazzling Gourmet
Winners Stores

*We gratefully acknowledge the following suppliers for their generous support of our Test and Photography Kitchens:*

*Broil King Barbecues*          *Hamilton Beach® Canada*          *Proctor Silex® Canada*
*Corelle®*                      *Lagostina®*                      *Tupperware®*

**30-Minute Rookie Cook**

First Printing September 2007

**Library and Archives Canada Cataloguing in Publication**
Paré, Jean, date-
30-minute rookie cook / Jean Paré.
(Original series)
Includes index.
ISBN 978-1-897069-29-5
1.  Quick and easy cookery. I. Title. II. Title: Thirty-minute rookie cook. III.  Series.
TX652.P376 2007       641.5'12       C2007-900756-2

Published by
**Company's Coming Publishing Limited**
2311 – 96 Street
Edmonton, Alberta, Canada T6N 1G3
Tel: 780-450-6223   Fax: 780-450-1857
www.companyscoming.com

We acknowledge the financial support of the Government of Canada through the
Book Publishing Industry Development Program (BPIDP) for our publishing activities.

Printed in China

# Need more recipes?

Six *"sneak preview"* recipes are featured online **with every new book released.**

Visit us at
### www.companyscoming.com

# Company's Coming Cookbooks

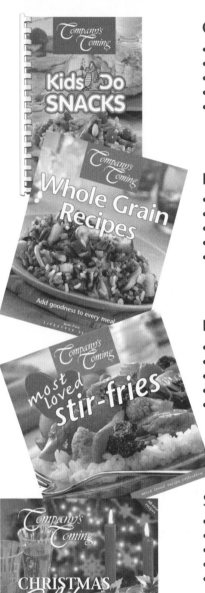

## Original Series

- Softcover, 160 pages
- 6" x 9" (15 cm x 23 cm) format
- Lay-flat plastic comb binding
- Full-colour photos
- Nutrition information

Quick & easy recipes! Everyday ingredients!

## Lifestyle Series

- Softcover, 160 pages
- 8" x 10" (20 cm x 25 cm) format
- Paperback
- Full-colour photos
- Nutrition information

## Most Loved Recipe Collection

- Hardcover, 128 pages
- 8 3/4" x 8 3/4" (22 cm x 22 cm) format
- Durable sewn binding
- Full-colour throughout
- Nutrition information

## Special Occasion Series

- Hardcover & softcover
- 8 1/2" x 11" (22 cm x 28 cm) format
- Durable sewn binding
- Full-colour throughout
- Nutrition information

**See page 157 for more cookbooks.**
**For a complete listing, visit**
**www.companyscoming.com**

# Table of Contents

The Company's Coming Story ........ 6

Foreword ...................... 7

Your Guide to Good Cooking......... 8

Appetizers
*to get the party started* ............. 16

Breakfasts & Lunches
*perfect whenever you get up.*......... 28

Salads & Soups
*when you want to lighten up your life.* . . 44

Sides
*'cause there's more to life than meat* ... 60

Go-Withs
*to add a special touch to your meal* .... 73

Mains
*and tonight's specials are...*
    Beef ......................... 84
    Chicken ..................... 96
    Fish & Seafood................ 109
    Meatless .................... 118
    Pork & Lamb ................. 127

Sweets & Treats
*consider it a well-earned reward*...... 136

Measurement Tables.............. 150

Coach Index ................... 151

Recipe Index................... 152

Mail Order Form................ 158

# The Company's Coming Story

Jean Paré (pronounced "jeen PAIR-ee") grew up understanding that the combination of family, friends and home cooking is the best recipe for a good life. From her mother, she learned to appreciate good cooking, while her father praised even her earliest attempts in the kitchen. When Jean left home, she took with her a love of cooking, many family recipes and an intriguing desire to read cookbooks as if they were novels!

*"never share a recipe you wouldn't use yourself"*

In 1963, when her four children had all reached school age, Jean volunteered to cater the 50th Anniversary of the Vermilion School of Agriculture, now Lakeland College, in Alberta, Canada. Working out of her home, Jean prepared a dinner for more than 1,000 people, which launched a flourishing catering operation that continued for over 18 years. During that time, she had countless opportunities to test new ideas with immediate feedback—resulting in empty plates and contented customers! Whether preparing cocktail sandwiches for a house party or serving a hot meal for 1,500 people, Jean Paré earned a reputation for good food, courteous service and reasonable prices.

As requests for her recipes mounted, Jean was often asked the question, "Why don't you write a cookbook?" Jean responded by teaming up with her son, Grant Lovig, in the fall of 1980 to form Company's Coming Publishing Limited. The publication of *150 Delicious Squares* on April 14, 1981 marked the debut of what would soon become one of the world's most popular cookbook series.

The company has grown since those early days when Jean worked from a spare bedroom in her home. Today, she continues to write recipes while working closely with the staff of the Recipe Factory, as the Company's Coming test kitchen is affectionately known. There she fills the role of mentor, assisting with the development of recipes people most want to use for everyday cooking and easy entertaining. Every Company's Coming recipe is *kitchen-tested* before it's approved for publication.

Jean's daughter, Gail Lovig, is responsible for marketing and distribution, leading a team that includes sales personnel located in major cities across Canada. In addition, Company's Coming cookbooks are published and distributed under licence in the United States, Australia and other world markets. Bestsellers many times over in English, Company's Coming cookbooks have also been published in French and Spanish.

Familiar and trusted in home kitchens around the world, Company's Coming cookbooks are offered in a variety of formats. Highly regarded as kitchen workbooks, the softcover Original Series, with its lay-flat plastic comb binding, is still a favourite among readers.

Jean Paré's approach to cooking has always called for *quick and easy recipes* using *everyday ingredients.* That view has served her well. The recipient of many awards, including the Queen Elizabeth Golden Jubilee medal, Jean was appointed a Member of the Order of Canada, her country's highest lifetime achievement honour.

Jean continues to gain new supporters by adhering to what she calls The Golden Rule of Cooking: *"Never share a recipe you wouldn't use yourself."* It's an approach that works— *millions of times over!*

# Foreword

In a world filled with fast-food restaurants and frozen dinners, it's easy to think a modern person can make it through life without ever really spending time in a kitchen.

We all know that today's world requires us to be on the run most of the time. A lot of on-the-go people like to say "I don't have time to cook," but the recipes in this book are designed to have you in the kitchen for only a short time. There's nothing wrong with eating on the go once in a while, but preparing (and then later enjoying) a great meal shouldn't be seen as a chore. It's something you can have fun with. Turn on your favourite music and think of the kitchen not as a place of work, but as a creative space. You'll find that you can create a wholesome meal in the time it takes to watch an episode of your favourite show.

Learning to cook is something you can do as you go—and it's certainly a lot more fun than doing your taxes! With some simple guidance, *30-Minute Rookie Cook* will help you make great meals without a great deal of trouble. Think of the pride you'll feel eating and sharing meals with your guests knowing that you've prepared them yourself. And, boy, are these recipes guest-worthy!

From impressive main dishes like Cheesy Portobellos, page 92, to sides like Cranberry Couscous, page 69, to desserts like Tiramisu Parfait, page 147, what guest wouldn't be pleased to accept your dinner invitation?

The recipes in this book were selected because they aren't complicated—they are designed to get novice cooks in the kitchen and creating meals in short order. No one expects you to put your life on hold as you learn how to cook. Instead, learn how easily cooking meals can fit into your busy schedule.

*Jean Paré*

---

### Nutrition Information Guidelines

Each recipe is analyzed using the most current version of the Canadian Nutrient File from Health Canada, which is based on the United States Department of Agriculture (USDA) Nutrient Database.

- If more than one ingredient is listed (such as "butter or hard margarine"), or if a range is given (1 – 2 tsp., 5 – 10 mL), only the first ingredient or first amount is analyzed.

- For meat, poultry and fish, the serving size per person is based on the recommended 4 oz. (113 g) uncooked weight (without bone), which is 2 – 3 oz. (57 – 85 g) cooked weight (without bone)—approximately the size of a deck of playing cards.

- Milk used is 1% M.F. (milk fat), unless otherwise stated.

- Cooking oil used is canola oil, unless otherwise stated.

- Ingredients indicating "sprinkle," "optional," or "for garnish" are not included in the nutrition information.

- The fat in recipes and combination foods can vary greatly depending on the sources and types of fats used in each specific ingredient. For these reasons, the amount of saturated, monounsaturated and polyunsaturated fats may not add up to the total fat content.

Vera C. Mazurak, Ph.D.
Nutritionist

# Your Guide to Good Cooking

## Before you begin

*Using recipes may seem pretty straightforward but there are a few tricks that make cooking so much easier:*

1. **Read the recipe.** You wouldn't believe how many people don't do this. Our recipes are organized in a very logical manner. The ingredients are listed in the order you need them, and the cooking method is listed in a step-by-step manner—this means you don't have to worry about jumping back and forth in the recipe to figure out what you should be doing when.
2. **Make sure you understand all the cooking terms used.** Before turning on a burner or preheating an oven, know what you have to do. If you're not sure what "simmer" means, look it up first in the handy glossary we've included. Using the wrong cooking method may result in a truly regrettable meal.
3. **Collect all the utensils you'll need before you start.** There's nothing worse than having something simmering on the stove and realizing you can't add that all-important ingredient because you can't remember where you've left the measuring cup, or perhaps you can't even remember if you own a measuring cup!
4. **Collect and prepare all your ingredients before starting.** Nothing's more annoying than being halfway through making a meal, shaking out a bag of flour, and finding you have a quarter cup less than you need. Avoid those emergency trips to the grocery store by thinking of a recipe as a checklist first, and a guide second.

# Tricky things about recipes

*Every single recipe in this book has been prepared, tested and evaluated in our Company's Coming test kitchen, so we know they work and we love the way they taste. That being said, sometimes things go wrong when people use different types of equipment or ingredients, so keep in mind the following:*

**All microwaves aren't created equal...and the same goes for ovens.** In the test kitchen, all our microwaves are 900 watts—but microwaves are sold in many different powers. You should be able to find the wattage of yours by opening the door and looking for the mandatory label. If your microwave is more than 900 watts, you may need to reduce the cooking time. If it's less than 900 watts, you'll probably need to increase the cooking time. The same goes for ovens—don't assume you can just put your food in for the maximum amount of time and everything will be fine.

**It's over when it's over...except when it isn't.** Many recipes will give time ranges for doneness ("bake for 25 to 35 minutes"). Make sure to check for doneness at the low end of the range (after 25 minutes). This will ensure that you are accounting for differences in ovens and microwaves and your food won't end up burned. In our recipes, we often give you hints as to when a product is done ("bake for 18 to 20 minutes until wooden pick inserted in centre of muffin comes out clean"). These clues will help you judge when your food is properly cooked. And if cooking meat makes you nervous, we highly recommend you invest in a meat thermometer that lists safe temperatures for cooking a variety of meats—it is the best way to make sure your meat will be safe to eat.

**Accept no substitutions...most of the time.** There are times when you may not have the exact ingredient and are wondering if the recipe will still work if you make a small substitution. In our books we often give you variations or suggestions for using different ingredients—whenever we do this, you'll be fine. In other cases, you're going to need to use common sense. For example, often it's OK to substitute frozen veggies for fresh—as long as they're thawed when you're ready to cook. But beware of replacing some ingredients with their "low-fat" or "light" varieties. Many low-fat products have higher water contents, which can mess with the final result—especially when it comes to baking.

# Food safety essentials

*With great cooking comes great responsibility. You don't want to be the person who gave all your dinner guests the extra gift of food poisoning at last week's get-together, so take care and heed the following points of advice:*

- **Juices from raw meat or poultry are dangerous**—they need to be cleaned up right away. Always clean with soap and water after you've used a counter. Don't let food stains set, because they get a lot harder to clean when they harden. If you do the little cleaning jobs as you go, you will save yourself from having to spend hours cleaning a kitchen that has been neglected.
- **Don't keep using the same sponges or dishcloths**—they can collect bacteria and actually spread it around, rather than clean it up. Use paper towels if you can. If you prefer to use sponges, change them often. It doesn't take long for a sponge to soak up a laboratory's worth of bacteria. If you want to use cloth towels, remember to wash them often in hot water. If your home washer has a "sanitary" setting, that's what you should use for kitchen towels.
- **Good cooks always keep themselves clean.** Have some antibacterial hand soap ready by the sink, and wash your hands regularly as you cook. This may sound basic, but it's amazing how many people will handle raw meat or poultry and then toss salad greens without washing their hands. The same goes for the cutting board. Don't cut vegetables on it right after you've been chopping chicken. Cross-contamination equals food poisoning. And make sure to wash your utensils and cooking implements between different ingredients!
- **Don't thaw meat on the counter.** Sure, it might seem a lot faster to defrost a frozen steak at room temperature, but the safe method is to do it in the refrigerator. And keep a dish under your meat to catch falling juices.

- **Refrigerate and/or freeze leftover items right away.** Don't add sour cream to a recipe and leave the remainder out on the counter for hours. Make sure it goes back in the refrigerator right away. Think of it this way: every second food is not refrigerated, it is spoiling—so get it back into the fridge right away. The same goes with freezing. If you plan to freeze uneaten portions of the dish you just made, do it as soon as possible. Leaving food out not only causes it to spoil but it can also attract vermin—and nobody wants to be the person with a pest problem in the kitchen.

## Time-saving strategies for easy cooking

*The recipes in this book were designed to be easy to finish and not keep you in the kitchen for a long time. But we understand that we all have those days where it's hard to spare even half an hour to make a meal. On those days that you do have a little bit of extra time, you can do the following prep work to ensure you won't be wasting time when you are in a rush:*

- Once a week, make sure to sit down and **plan meals** for the next seven days. From that list, make a list of grocery items you will need, and then do all the shopping in one fell swoop. This will save you from having to run to the grocery store every day.

- **Keep a running list of essentials** (such as sugar, flour and salt) on your refrigerator door. As soon as one of these items runs low, make a note of it so you will know to add it to your shopping list for the week. Keeping the kitchen well-stocked is the key to saving time.

- If you know you'll be hitting a spot where you will be pressed for time, working longer hours or have lots of family commitments, **make extra when you are cooking.** That way you can freeze the remainder and heat it up later. You can also take those extra meal portions to work with you. Not only will you get some comfort food at work, you'll save your money, too.

## Items for a practical pantry

*Below, we've listed the most common non-perishable or long-lasting items we've used in this book. They're great staples to have around the house for last-minute cooking. Often these items go on sale, so you can purchase them when the prices suit your pocketbook. And as far as the spices go, we suggest you buy small amounts of bulk spices and put them in small, labelled airtight containers. Buying spices this way costs a fraction of what buying bottles of spices costs.*

**Canned items**
- beans • fruit • soup • vegetables

**Dry items**
- baking powder • baking soda • bread crumbs • cornstarch
- graham cracker crumbs • long grain rice • pasta and noodles

**Oils, etc.**
- cooking oil (we use canola oil) • olive oil • cooking spray

**Spices, herbs & seasonings**
- Cajun seasoning • cayenne pepper • chili powder • curry powder
- dried basil • dried crushed chilies • dried dillweed • dried oregano
- dried rosemary • dried thyme • dry mustard • garlic powder
- ground allspice • ground cinnamon • ground cloves • ground ginger
- ground nutmeg • Italian seasoning • lemon pepper
- Montreal steak spice • onion powder • paprika • parsley flakes
- poultry seasoning • seasoned salt • sesame seeds • taco seasoning

**Miscellaneous**
- barbecue sauce • basil pesto • chili paste (sambal oelek) • chili sauce
- cocoa powder • fancy mild molasses • hoisin sauce • honey
- hot pepper sauce • jams • ketchup • mango chutney • mayonnaise
- mustard • nuts • peanut butter • pizza, pasta & tomato sauces
- prepared beef broth • prepared chicken broth • salad dressings
- salsa • soy sauce • sun-dried tomato pesto • sweet chili sauce
- thick teriyaki basting sauce • tomato paste • vanilla extract
- white vinegar • Worcestershire sauce

# Essential kitchen equipment

Baking dish (glass) pan (metal) | Baking sheet | Blender or food processor | Bowls (mixing) | Bread knife

Broiler pan | Brush | Can opener | Casserole | Colander

Cookie sheet | Cutting board | Dry measures | Dutch oven | Electric mixer

Frying pan | Grater | Liquid measures | Measuring spoons | Meat thermometer

Mixing spoon | Muffin pan and mini-muffin pan | Pancake lifter | Pie plate | Pizza pan

Potato masher | Rubber spatula | Saucepan | Sharp knife | Sieve

Square baking pan | Vegetable peeler | Whisk | Wire rack | Wok

**13**

# Cooking glossary

*Below, we've compiled a list of cooking terms you may not be familiar with. The good thing with cooking is that the basic techniques are used over and over again—so the more you cook, the more your cooking knowledge will increase.*

**Batter:** A thick or thin uncooked, pourable mixture.

**Beat:** Mixing or stirring ingredients together as rapidly as possible. You can do this manually or with an electric mixer.

**Blot:** Using a paper towel to absorb liquid from ingredients or to remove fat from fried food.

**Broil:** This is cooking using direct, high heat in an oven. The heat always comes from an overhead source. Every oven has a "broil" setting. You may be asked to move your oven rack closer to the top element so the food is nearer to the heat source. It is customary to leave your oven open a crack when broiling to prevent the food from baking.

**Brown:** This is the process of cooking an item in a greased pan so it quickly forms a brown crust which locks in flavour and juices. After a meat is browned, it will then be thoroughly cooked using a different cooking method.

**Chop:** A method of cutting food where the ingredient is cut into several pieces. The pieces do not necessarily have to be uniform, but they shouldn't vary greatly in size.

**Cut in:** When adding butter (or another solid fat) to a dry mixture, use a pastry blender or two knives to mix the butter only to the point where it is evenly spread through the ingredients. The butter or fat should be broken into small crumb-like pieces, with each piece totally covered in the dry ingredients.

**Dice:** This is the process of cutting food into small, equally-sized cube-shaped pieces. Dicing ensures even cooking of each morsel.

**Doneness:** When any food item is cooked well enough so it is safe to eat, it is "done." With meat, "doneness" can also indicate at what stage the diner prefers to eat the meat—rare, medium, well done, etc.

**Drain:** The removal of liquid or fat from food. The easiest way to drain food is to use a colander or mesh sieve.

**Drippings:** These are the juices that gather in the pan during the cooking of meat. The drippings can be used to make gravy or to fry other foods.

**Drizzle:** This is the process of pouring a very small amount of sauce, liquid or melted butter over food.

**Fork-beaten:** Using a fork to rapidly break up an ingredient.

**Garnish:** A garnish is an edible item, such as a fruit or an herb, that is added to a finished dish as a decoration.

**Grate:** A method of cutting by sliding a piece of solid food, usually cheese or a vegetable, against a grater. Graters may be sold with different holes and slots which produce different sizes of gratings from coarse to fine.

**Grease:** Applying a fat (such as cooking spray or butter) in a thin layer on a cooking surface before it is heated to prevent the food from sticking to the pan.

**Halftime:** The halfway point of the cooking process. In a lot of recipes, you will be asked to turn, check or add something to the food at halftime.

**Jelly-roll style:** You may be asked to roll flatter items in this manner. It simply means starting from one end and rolling while keeping the edges even.

**Knead:** The process of working dough into a smooth, putty-like mass by pressing down and folding in using the heels of your hands.

**Let stand:** If a recipe tells you to let something stand after cooking, simply place the food on a wire rack and leave it for the allotted time. Baked goods often need to stand so they don't lose their shape.

**Mince:** This is the process of cutting or grinding food into tiny pieces—usually much smaller than an 1/8 inch (3 mm) each.

**Pinch:** An amount of a dry ingredient that is too small to measure. A "pinch" is literally just that—use just what will fit in between your finger and thumb, and sprinkle it on the mixture.

**Preheat:** The turning on of an oven before food is placed in it. This is done so the oven can reach the cooking temperature specified in the recipe by the time the pan is ready to go in.

**Process:** Mixing or cutting up food using a blender or food processor.

**Scramble-fry:** To cook an item in a frying pan on medium or medium-high heat by continuously breaking it apart and redistributing it throughout the pan with a fork or a spatula.

**Sift:** This is the process of shaking dry ingredients through a fine mesh sieve to remove any lumps.

**Simmer:** After an item starts to boil, the heat is turned down to a medium-low temperature where it can gently bubble and continue to cook.

**Slice:** To cut food items, like apples or bread, into thinner portions.

**Soften:** Harder ingredients, like butter, may need to be softened so they're easier to work with. Soften by placing the ingredient on the counter, at room temperature, for about half an hour or microwaving for approximately 10 seconds.

**Split:** To cut items, usually buns or bread, straight down the middle, separating them into two halves.

**Stir-fry:** To cook food quickly in a hot frying pan or wok while stirring continuously.

**Whisk:** To mix ingredients using a whisk—a special wire instrument. Whisking is also a great way to break up lumps in dry ingredients.

**15**

# Tropical Shrimp Dip

*Send your taste buds to the tropics with this elegant dip that's*
*perfect for your poshest company. Serve with rice crackers.*

| | | |
|---|---|---|
| Butter (or hard margarine) | 1 tbsp. | 15 mL |
| Garlic clove, minced | 1 | 1 |
| (or 1/4 tsp., 1 mL, powder) | | |
| Bag of frozen, uncooked shrimp (peeled and deveined), thawed and chopped | 3/4 lb. | 340 g |
| Can of pineapple tidbits, drained | 14 oz. | 398 mL |
| Barbecue sauce | 1/3 cup | 75 mL |
| Half-and-half cream | 1/4 cup | 60 mL |
| Medium unsweetened coconut | 3 tbsp. | 50 mL |
| Cayenne pepper | 1/8 tsp. | 0.5 mL |
| Chopped fresh parsley | 1 tbsp. | 15 mL |

Melt butter in large frying pan on medium. Add garlic. Heat and stir for about 30 seconds until fragrant. Add shrimp. Heat and stir for about 1 minute until shrimp start to turn pink.

Add next 5 ingredients. Heat and stir for 1 to 2 minutes until hot and shrimp are pink. Do not overcook. Transfer to blender or food processor. Process with on/off motion until coarsely chopped. Transfer to serving bowl.

Sprinkle with parsley. Makes about 3 cups (750 mL).

*1/4 cup (60 mL): 80 Calories; 3.3 g Total Fat (0.6 g Mono, 0.3 g Poly, 2.1 g Sat); 46 mg Cholesterol; 7 g Carbohydrate; 1 g Fibre; 6 g Protein; 104 mg Sodium*

1. Speedy Sassy Salsa, page 79
2. Mega Meatball Sandwiches, page 88
3. Pecan Raisin Tarts, page 139

Props courtesy of: Pier 1 Imports
The Bay
Winners Stores

# Shrimp Crostini

*These crisp little toasts topped with a spicy, sweet and tangy shrimp mixture are highly addictive. If you're a fan of spice, be sure to double the amount of chili paste.*

| | | |
|---|---|---|
| Baguette bread slices (1/4 inch, 6 mm, thick) | 48 | 48 |
| Cooking oil | 1 tbsp. | 15 mL |
| Frozen, cooked shrimp (peeled and deveined), thawed and finely chopped | 1/4 lb. | 113 g |
| Finely chopped yellow pepper | 1/4 cup | 60 mL |
| Seafood cocktail sauce | 1/4 cup | 60 mL |
| Finely chopped green onion | 3 tbsp. | 50 mL |
| Chili paste (sambal oelek) | 1/2 tsp. | 2 mL |

Preheat oven to 400°F (205°C). Arrange baguette slices in single layer on ungreased baking sheet with sides. Lightly brush tops of baguette slices with cooking oil. Bake for about 10 minutes, turning at halftime, until golden and crisp.

Meanwhile, combine remaining 5 ingredients in small bowl. Spoon onto baguette slices. Makes 48 crostini.

*1 crostini: 148 Calories; 0.8 g Total Fat (0.1 g Mono, 0.1 g Poly, trace Sat); 4 mg Cholesterol; 28 g Carbohydrate; 1 g Fibre; 5 g Protein; 361 mg Sodium*

Pictured on page 18.

1. Brie Happy, page 21
2. Cucumber Hummus Rounds, page 20
3. Shrimp Crostini, above

Props courtesy of: Winners Stores

# Green Olive Tapenade

*Everyone will be green with envy when they see what a great cook you've become. Serve as a dip or as a spread for crackers or bread.*

| | | |
|---|---|---|
| Large pitted green olives | 1 cup | 250 mL |
| Pine nuts, toasted (see Coach, page 63) | 3 tbsp. | 50 mL |
| Garlic cloves (or 1/2 tsp., 2 mL, powder) | 2 | 2 |
| Dried oregano | 1 tsp. | 5 mL |
| Ground cumin | 1/4 tsp. | 1 mL |
| Pepper | 1/4 tsp. | 1 mL |
| Olive (or cooking) oil | 1/4 cup | 60 mL |
| Turmeric | 1/4 tsp. | 1 mL |

Put first 6 ingredients into blender or food processor. Process until finely chopped.

Add olive oil and turmeric. Process until just combined. Transfer to small bowl. Makes about 1 cup (250 mL).

*2 tbsp. (30 mL): 123 Calories; 12.6 g Total Fat (8.7 g Mono, 2.4 g Poly, 1.2 g Sat); 0 mg Cholesterol; 3 g Carbohydrate; 1 g Fibre; 1 g Protein; 469 mg Sodium*

# Cucumber Hummus Rounds

*Set your taste buds a-hummin' with this easy appetizer. Hummus is quite a different taste experience when paired with tangy yogurt and crisp, cool cucumber. Use your favourite flavour of hummus—roasted red pepper is what we used.*

| | | |
|---|---|---|
| English cucumber slices (with peel), 1/4 inch (6 mm) thick | 30 | 30 |
| Salt, sprinkle | | |
| Hummus | 2/3 cup | 150 mL |
| Plain yogurt | 2/3 cup | 150 mL |
| Sesame seeds, toasted (see Coach, page 63) | 1 tbsp. | 15 mL |

Arrange cucumber slices on serving platter. Sprinkle with salt.

*(continued on next page)*

**20**

Appetizers

Spoon 1 tsp. (5 mL) hummus onto each cucumber slice. Spread evenly.

Spoon 1 tsp. (5 mL) yogurt over hummus on each slice. Sprinkle with sesame seeds. Makes 30 rounds.

*1 round: 33 Calories; 1.2 g Total Fat (0.2 g Mono, 0.2 g Poly, 0.3 g Sat); 1 mg Cholesterol; 5 g Carbohydrate; 1 g Fibre; 2 g Protein; 25 mg Sodium*

Pictured on page 18.

---

# Brie Happy

*What's not to Brie happy about? It's so easy to prepare this trendy dish. Serve with slices of apple, grapes or crackers. If you're really rushed, heat on medium power in the microwave for about two minutes.*

| | | |
|---|---|---|
| Brie cheese round | 4 oz. | 125 g |
| Apricot jam | 2 tbsp. | 30 mL |
| Brown sugar, packed | 1 1/2 tsp. | 7 mL |
| Grated orange zest | 1/4 tsp. | 1 mL |
| Ground cinnamon | 1/8 tsp. | 0.5 mL |
| Sliced almonds, toasted (see Coach, page 63) | 1 tbsp. | 15 mL |

Preheat oven to 325°F (160°C). Remove and discard rind from top of cheese. Place cheese round in small shallow baking dish.

Combine next 4 ingredients in small bowl. Spoon over cheese round. Bake for 10 to 12 minutes until cheese is softened and warm.

Sprinkle almonds over top. Serves 4.

*1 serving: 127 Calories; 8.0 g Total Fat (2.7 g Mono, 0.5 g Poly, 4.4 g Sat); 25 mg Cholesterol; 9 g Carbohydrate; trace Fibre; 6 g Protein; 161 mg Sodium*

Pictured on page 18.

COACH

Customize your Brie with your favourite flavours by trying other jams or jellies in place of the apricot jam. Apple or jalapeño jelly work great!

# Beef-Stuffed Mushrooms

*These two-bite mushrooms won't have your dinner guests too stuffed to indulge in your main course—but it may be hard to limit them to only a few!*

| Medium fresh whole white mushrooms | 36 | 36 |
|---|---|---|
| Cooking oil | 1/2 tsp. | 2 mL |
| Lean ground beef | 1/4 lb. | 113 g |
| Finely chopped onion | 1/4 cup | 60 mL |
| Ketchup | 1 tbsp. | 15 mL |
| Prepared horseradish | 1 1/4 tsp. | 6 mL |
| Celery salt | 1/4 tsp. | 1 mL |
| Garlic powder | 1/4 tsp. | 1 mL |
| Salt | 1/4 tsp. | 1 mL |
| Pepper | 1/8 tsp. | 0.5 mL |
| Grated Parmesan cheese | 3 tbsp. | 50 mL |

Preheat broiler. Remove stems from mushrooms. Finely chop stems. Set aside. Arrange mushroom caps on ungreased baking sheet with sides. Broil on top rack in oven for about 3 minutes per side until browned. Set aside.

Preheat oven to 400°F (205°C). Heat cooking oil in large frying pan on medium-high. Add beef, onion and mushroom stems. Scramble-fry for about 5 minutes until beef is no longer pink. Drain.

Add next 6 ingredients. Stir. Spoon about 1/2 tsp. (2 mL) beef mixture into each mushroom cap.

Sprinkle with cheese. Bake for about 10 minutes until heated through. Makes 36 stuffed mushrooms.

*1 stuffed mushroom: 24 Calories; 1.1 g Total Fat (0.4 g Mono, 0.1 g Poly, 0.6 g Sat); 4 mg Cholesterol; 1 g Carbohydrate; trace Fibre; 2 g Protein; 79 mg Sodium*

Only wash your mushrooms prior to using. You can use a special mushroom brush to gently remove any dirt and then quickly rinse under water. Don't have a mushroom brush? A soft-bristled toothbrush works just as well.

# Tuna Bruschetta

*Tuna adds a rather sophisticated dimension to bruschetta—
your guests will be pleasantly surprised.*

| | | |
|---|---|---|
| Olive (or cooking) oil | 3 tbsp. | 50 mL |
| Garlic cloves, minced | 2 | 2 |
| (or 1/2 tsp., 2 mL, powder) | | |
| Baguette bread slices | 48 | 48 |
| (1/2 inch, 12 mm, thick) | | |
| Can of chunk light tuna in water, drained | 6 oz. | 170 g |
| Finely chopped red onion | 1/2 cup | 125 mL |
| Large tomato, quartered, seeds removed, | 1 | 1 |
| finely chopped | | |
| Finely chopped dill pickle | 3 tbsp. | 50 mL |
| Chopped fresh dill | 2 tbsp. | 30 mL |
| (or 1 1/2 tsp., 7 mL, dried) | | |
| Lemon juice | 2 tbsp. | 30 mL |
| Creamed horseradish | 1 tbsp. | 15 mL |
| Olive (or cooking) oil | 2 tsp. | 10 mL |
| Salt | 1/4 tsp. | 1 mL |
| Pepper | 1/4 tsp. | 1 mL |

Preheat broiler. Combine first amount of olive oil and garlic in small cup.
Brush on both sides of each baguette slice. Arrange in single layer on
ungreased baking sheet with sides. Broil on top rack in oven for about
1 minute per side until golden.

Combine remaining 10 ingredients in medium bowl. Spoon onto baguette
slices. Makes 48 bruschetta.

*1 bruschetta: 155 Calories; 1.6 g Total Fat (0.8 g Mono, 0.1 g Poly, 0.2 g Sat); 1 mg Cholesterol;
29 g Carbohydrate; 1 g Fibre; 6 g Protein; 357 mg Sodium*

**COACH**

If your oven is full of other appies and you can't
dedicate the toasting time, use pre-made crostini
instead of baguette slices.

# Ham And Cheese Spirals

*It won't be the swirly-twirly design that hypnotizes your guests,*
*it'll be the sublime savoury, yet sweet, taste.*

| | | |
|---|---|---|
| Cream cheese, softened | 4 oz. | 125 g |
| Grated carrot | 1/4 cup | 60 mL |
| Ranch dressing | 1/4 cup | 60 mL |
| Flour tortillas (9 inch, 22 cm, diameter) | 4 | 4 |
| Deli ham slices (about 7 oz., 200 g) | 4 | 4 |

Mash cream cheese with fork in small bowl. Add carrot and dressing. Stir well.

Spread cream cheese mixture evenly over each tortilla, almost to edge.

Place 1 ham slice over cream cheese mixture on each tortilla. Roll up tightly, jelly-roll style. Trim ends. Cut each roll diagonally into 8 slices. Makes 32 slices.

*1 slice: 41 Calories; 2.7 g Total Fat (0.4 g Mono, 0.1 g Poly, 1.1 g Sat); 6 mg Cholesterol; 3 g Carbohydrate; trace Fibre; 1 g Protein; 106 mg Sodium*

---

# Bacon Mushroom Dip

*If you're achin' for bacon, this is the dip for you. With bits of crisp bacon*
*and fried mushrooms, it goes great with raw vegetables or potato skins.*

| | | |
|---|---|---|
| Bacon slices, diced | 2 | 2 |
| Finely chopped fresh white mushrooms | 1 cup | 250 mL |
| Sour cream | 1 cup | 250 mL |
| Mayonnaise | 1/4 cup | 60 mL |
| Finely chopped green onion | 1 tbsp. | 15 mL |
| Worcestershire sauce | 1 tsp. | 5 mL |

Cook bacon in medium frying pan on medium for about 5 minutes until crisp. Transfer with slotted spoon to paper towel-lined plate to drain. Set aside.

*(continued on next page)*

Appetizers

Heat 1 tsp. (5 mL) drippings in same frying pan on medium. Add mushrooms. Cook for about 3 minutes, stirring occasionally, until liquid is evaporated. Spread mushrooms evenly on plate to cool.

Combine remaining 4 ingredients in medium bowl. Add bacon and mushrooms. Stir well. Makes about 1 1/2 cups (375 mL).

*2 tbsp. (30 mL): 69 Calories; 6.3 g Total Fat (2.5 g Mono, 1.0 g Poly, 2.5 g Sat); 10 mg Cholesterol; 2 g Carbohydrate; trace Fibre; 1 g Protein; 66 mg Sodium*

# Chipotle Meatballs

*Meatballs are surprisingly successful cocktail fare, and the smoky, sweet and spicy sauce they're coated in is sure to be a hit.*

| | | |
|---|---|---|
| Box of frozen cooked meatballs | 2 1/4 lbs. | 1 kg |
| Salsa | 2 cups | 500 mL |
| Seedless raspberry jam | 1 cup | 250 mL |
| Coarsely chopped chipotle peppers in adobo sauce (see Coach, page 133) | 2 tsp. | 10 mL |
| Adobo sauce from chipotle peppers | 1 tsp. | 5 mL |
| Dried thyme | 1/2 tsp. | 2 mL |
| Chopped fresh parsley | 1 tbsp. | 15 mL |

Put meatballs into Dutch oven. Heat on high for 2 minutes.

Meanwhile, put next 5 ingredients into blender or food processor. Process until smooth. Add to meatballs. Stir until coated. Bring to a boil. Reduce heat to medium. Boil gently, covered, for about 20 minutes, stirring often, until heated through. Transfer to serving bowl.

Sprinkle with parsley. Makes about 75 meatballs.

*1 meatball: 41 Calories; 1.8 g Total Fat (0.8 g Mono, 0.1 g Poly, 0.6 g Sat); 11 mg Cholesterol; 4 g Carbohydrate; trace Fibre; 2 g Protein; 61 mg Sodium*

COACH

Serve your meatball appetizers with cocktail picks or toothpicks so your guests can eat them without having to use a fork.

# Baja Bean Dip

*This bean dip is unexpectedly refreshing. Smooth and creamy,*
*it goes especially well with crisp veggies or tortilla chips.*

| | | |
|---|---|---|
| Can of white kidney beans, rinsed and drained | 19 oz. | 540 mL |
| Chopped fresh cilantro or parsley | 1/4 cup | 60 mL |
| Olive (or cooking) oil | 3 tbsp. | 50 mL |
| Lime juice | 2 tbsp. | 30 mL |
| Finely chopped fresh jalapeño pepper (see Coach, page 75) | 1 tbsp. | 15 mL |
| Ground cumin | 1 tsp. | 5 mL |
| Dried oregano | 1/2 tsp. | 2 mL |
| Salt | 1/2 tsp. | 2 mL |
| Pepper | 1/2 tsp. | 2 mL |

Sprig of fresh cilantro or parsley, for garnish

Put first 9 ingredients into blender or food processor. Process, scraping down sides if necessary, until smooth. Transfer to serving bowl.

Garnish with cilantro sprig. Makes about 1 3/4 cups (425 mL).

*1/4 cup (60 mL): 112 Calories; 6.4 g Total Fat (4.2 g Mono, 0.5 g Poly, 0.8 g Sat); 0 mg Cholesterol; 11 g Carbohydrate; 3 g Fibre; 4 g Protein; 189 mg Sodium*

# Red Hot Chicken Bites

*Rather than going down to the pub to watch the next big game,*
*why not bake up a batch of these fiery snacks and invite the gang to your place?*
*Ranch dressing for dipping and a cold beer to wash them down are optional—*
*but definitely recommended!*

| | | |
|---|---|---|
| Grated Parmesan cheese | 6 tbsp. | 100 mL |
| Fine dry bread crumbs | 1/4 cup | 60 mL |
| Cajun seasoning | 1/2 tsp. | 2 mL |
| Garlic powder | 1/4 tsp. | 1 mL |
| Boneless, skinless chicken thighs, cut into bite-sized pieces | 3/4 lb. | 340 g |
| Louisiana hot sauce | 2 tbsp. | 30 mL |

*(continued on next page)*

Preheat oven to 375°F (190°C). Combine first 4 ingredients in medium bowl.

Put chicken into separate medium bowl. Drizzle hot sauce over top. Stir until coated. Add to crumb mixture in 3 batches. Toss until coated. Arrange in single layer on greased baking sheet with sides. Bake for about 20 minutes, turning at halftime, until golden and no longer pink inside. Makes about 30 delicious bites for the whole gang.

*1 bite: 55 Calories; 3.1 g Total Fat (1.1 g Mono, 0.3 g Poly, 1.5 g Sat); 16 mg Cholesterol; 1 g Carbohydrate; trace Fibre; 6 g Protein; 165 mg Sodium*

---

# Fire-Spiced Hot Wings

*Watch out, folks: we aren't kidding, these babies are hot! Arm yourself with a whole bunch of napkins and something to cool the fiery heat.*

| | | |
|---|---|---|
| Louisiana hot sauce | 1/3 cup | 75 mL |
| Lime juice | 1/4 cup | 60 mL |
| Soy sauce | 1/4 cup | 60 mL |
| Pepper | 1 tsp. | 5 mL |
| Cayenne pepper | 1/2 tsp. | 2 mL |
| Garlic powder | 1/2 tsp. | 2 mL |
| Split chicken wings, tips discarded (or chicken drumettes) | 2 lbs. | 900 g |

Preheat oven to 450°F (230°C). Combine first 6 ingredients in 1 cup (250 mL) liquid measure. Transfer 1/3 cup (75 mL) to small bowl. Set aside.

Put wing pieces into large resealable freezer bag. Add remaining hot sauce mixture. Seal bag. Toss until coated. Drain. Arrange wing pieces on greased wire rack set in foil-lined baking sheet with sides. Bake for about 15 minutes, turning at halftime, until tender and no longer pink inside. Remove from oven. Preheat broiler. Brush wing pieces with reserved hot sauce mixture. Broil on centre rack in oven for about 4 minutes until browned. Makes about 24 wing pieces (or 16 drumettes).

*1 wing: 116 Calories; 8.2 g Total Fat (3.1 g Mono, 2.1 g Poly, 2.1 g Sat); 31 mg Cholesterol; trace Carbohydrate; trace Fibre; 10 g Protein; 33 mg Sodium*

# Orange Chipper Muffins

*You'll be feeling rather chipper yourself after you try these muffins—the flavours
of orange and chocolate pair perfectly. Your blender will make quick work
of chopping the orange—and adding the peel gives extra health benefits.*

| | | |
|---|---|---|
| All-purpose flour | 2 cups | 500 mL |
| Cocoa, sifted if lumpy | 1 tbsp. | 15 mL |
| Baking powder | 1 1/2 tsp. | 7 mL |
| Baking soda | 1 tsp. | 5 mL |
| Salt | 1/4 tsp. | 1 mL |
| Large unpeeled orange, cut into eight wedges, seeds removed | 1 | 1 |
| Large eggs | 2 | 2 |
| Granulated sugar | 1 cup | 250 mL |
| Butter (or hard margarine), softened | 1/2 cup | 125 mL |
| Mini semi-sweet chocolate chips | 3/4 cup | 175 mL |

Preheat oven to 375°F (190°C). Measure first 5 ingredients into large bowl.
Stir. Make a well in centre.

Put orange wedges into blender or food processor. Process with on/off
motion until finely chopped. Add next 3 ingredients. Process until smooth.
Add to well.

Add chocolate chips. Stir until just moistened. Fill 12 greased muffin cups
3/4 full. Bake for 18 to 20 minutes until wooden pick inserted in centre
of muffin comes out clean. Let stand in pan for 5 minutes. Remove muffins
from pan and place on wire rack to cool. Makes 12 muffins.

*1 muffin: 287 Calories; 12.5 g Total Fat (3.7 g Mono, 0.6 g Poly, 7.6 g Sat); 51 mg Cholesterol;
42 g Carbohydrate; 2 g Fibre; 4 g Protein; 251 mg Sodium*

To avoid tough muffins, don't overmix the batter.
Overmixing will give the muffin a heavier bread-like
texture rather than the nice crumbly texture you'd expect.

# Protein Power Shake

*Energy abounds with these peachy protein-packed shakes!*

| | | |
|---|---|---|
| Can of sliced peaches in light syrup (with syrup) | 14 oz. | 398 mL |
| Milk | 1 cup | 250 mL |
| Package of peach dessert tofu | 5 1/3 oz. | 150 g |
| Liquid honey | 1 tbsp. | 15 mL |
| Vanilla extract (optional) | 1/4 tsp. | 1 mL |

Put all 5 ingredients into blender. Process until smooth. Makes about
3 1/2 cups (875 mL).

*1 cup (250 mL): 172 Calories; 1.6 g Total Fat (0.3 g Mono, 0.1 g Poly, 0.5 g Sat); 4 mg Cholesterol;
38 g Carbohydrate; 2 g Fibre; 5 g Protein; 48 mg Sodium*

# Pepperoni Pizza Bagels

*Use your favourite pizza toppings to customize this bagel beauty.*

| | | |
|---|---|---|
| Pizza sauce | 2 tbsp. | 30 mL |
| Plain bagel, split | 1 | 1 |
| Grated mozzarella cheese | 1/3 cup | 75 mL |
| Chopped pepperoni | 3 tbsp. | 50 mL |

Preheat oven to 400°F (205°C). Spread pizza sauce evenly over cut sides
of bagel. Place, cut-side up, on greased baking sheet with sides.

Sprinkle cheese over sauce. Sprinkle pepperoni over top. Bake for about
10 minutes until cheese is melted and bubbly. Makes 2 pizza bagels.

*1 pizza bagel: 291 Calories; 14.6 g Total Fat (5.9 g Mono, 1.4 g Poly, 6.1 g Sat); 32 mg Cholesterol;
26 g Carbohydrate; 1 g Fibre; 13 g Protein; 811 mg Sodium*

COACH

Freeze leftover pizza sauce in ice cube trays (about 2 tbsp.,
30 mL, sauce in each) to use at another time.

# Brunch Special

*Although this special treat would be perfect served on Christmas morn, its decadent, creamy sauce and the combination of scrambled eggs, ham and asparagus will make any morning a special occasion.*

| | | |
|---|---|---|
| Large eggs | 8 | 8 |
| Milk | 1/4 cup | 60 mL |
| Can of condensed cream of asparagus soup | 10 oz. | 284 mL |
| Milk | 1/2 cup | 125 mL |
| Butter (or hard margarine) | 1 tbsp. | 15 mL |
| Chopped fresh asparagus | 1 cup | 250 mL |
| Diced cooked ham | 1 cup | 250 mL |
| Plain English muffins, split | 4 | 4 |
| Grated medium Cheddar cheese | 1/2 cup | 125 mL |

Beat eggs and first amount of milk in small bowl. Set aside.

Combine soup and second amount of milk in small saucepan. Heat on medium for about 5 minutes, stirring often, until hot but not boiling. Cover to keep warm.

Meanwhile, melt butter in large frying pan on medium. Add asparagus and ham. Heat and stir for about 3 minutes until asparagus is tender-crisp. Add egg mixture. Cook for about 4 minutes, stirring constantly with spatula and scraping sides and bottom of pan, until eggs are set and liquid is evaporated. Stir in soup mixture.

Toast English muffins halves. Spoon egg mixture over muffin halves.

Sprinkle with cheese. Serves 4.

*1 serving: 539 Calories; 29.0 g Total Fat (9.2 g Mono, 2.3 g Poly, 11.5 g Sat); 432 mg Cholesterol; 36 g Carbohydrate; 3 g Fibre; 34 g Protein; 950 mg Sodium*

Pictured on page 41.

# Curried Waldorf Chicken Wraps

*If you're too wrapped up to step out and grab lunch, make this super-quick wrap instead! This also works great as appetizer fare—simply stuff the filling into small pitas.*

| | | |
|---|---|---|
| Mayonnaise | 1/2 cup | 125 mL |
| Lemon juice | 2 tsp. | 10 mL |
| Curry powder | 1/2 tsp. | 2 mL |
| Grated lemon zest | 1/2 tsp. | 2 mL |
| Salt | 1/4 tsp. | 1 mL |
| Pepper | 1/4 tsp. | 1 mL |
| Chopped cooked chicken (see Coach, below) | 2 cups | 500 mL |
| Chopped unpeeled apple | 1 cup | 250 mL |
| Chopped celery | 3/4 cup | 175 mL |
| Chopped walnuts | 1/4 cup | 60 mL |
| Lettuce leaves | 6 | 6 |
| Flour tortillas (9 inch, 22 cm, diameter) | 6 | 6 |

Combine first 6 ingredients in medium bowl.

Add next 4 ingredients. Stir until coated.

Place 1 lettuce leaf on each tortilla. Spoon chicken mixture down centre of leaves. Fold bottom ends of tortillas over filling. Fold in sides, slightly overlapping, leaving top ends open. Place, seam-side down, on plate. Makes 6 wraps.

*1 wrap: 389 Calories; 21.3 g Total Fat (7.4 g Mono, 6.6 g Poly, 3.2 g Sat); 49 mg Cholesterol; 32 g Carbohydrate; 2 g Fibre; 19 g Protein; 587 mg Sodium*

COACH

Don't have any leftover chicken? Start with two boneless, skinless chicken breast halves (4 – 6 oz., 113 – 170 g, each). Place in a large frying pan with 1 cup (250 mL) water or chicken broth. Simmer, covered, for 12 to 14 minutes until no longer pink inside. Drain. Chop. Makes about 2 cups (500 mL) of cooked chicken.

# Denver Noodle Frittata

*A noodle frittata? It works! Noodles add texture
to this familiar-tasting, family-friendly frittata.*

| | | |
|---|---|---|
| Water | 4 cups | 1 L |
| Salt | 1/2 tsp. | 2 mL |
| Tiny shell pasta | 1 cup | 250 mL |
| Cooking oil | 1 tbsp. | 15 mL |
| Diced cooked ham | 3/4 cup | 175 mL |
| Chopped green pepper | 1/2 cup | 125 mL |
| Chopped onion | 1/2 cup | 125 mL |
| Large eggs | 6 | 6 |
| Salt | 1/4 tsp. | 1 mL |
| Cayenne pepper | 1/8 tsp. | 0.5 mL |
| Grated medium Cheddar cheese | 1 cup | 250 mL |
| Chopped fresh parsley | 1 tbsp. | 15 mL |

Combine water and salt in medium saucepan. Bring to a boil. Add pasta. Boil, uncovered, for 6 to 8 minutes, stirring occasionally, until tender but firm. Drain. Return to same pot. Cover to keep warm.

Meanwhile, heat cooking oil in medium frying pan on medium. Add next 3 ingredients. Cook for about 5 minutes, stirring occasionally, until onion is tender-crisp. Add pasta. Stir. Spread evenly in pan.

Preheat broiler. Beat next 3 ingredients with fork in medium bowl. Pour over pasta mixture. Reduce heat to medium-low. Cook, covered, for about 5 minutes until bottom is golden and top is almost set. Remove from heat.

Sprinkle cheese over top. Broil on centre rack in oven (see Coach, page 95) for 2 to 4 minutes until cheese is melted and golden.

Sprinkle with parsley. Cuts into 4 wedges.

*1 wedge:* 544 Calories; 25.5 g Total Fat (9.9 g Mono, 2.8 g Poly, 10.4 g Sat); 332 mg Cholesterol; 47 g Carbohydrate; 2 g Fibre; 31 g Protein; 432 mg Sodium

Pictured on page 35.

# Turkey Pita

*Get fresh pitas from the local Lebanese or Greek bakery*
*to use in this tasty wrap. A great lunch to take to work or school—*
*just remember to keep it cool until you're ready to eat.*

| | | |
|---|---|---|
| Salad dressing (or mayonnaise) | 1 tbsp. | 15 mL |
| Sun-dried tomato pesto | 1 tsp. | 5 mL |
| Pita bread (7 inch, 18 cm, diameter) | 1 | 1 |
| Lettuce leaves | 4 | 4 |
| Grated medium Cheddar cheese | 1/4 cup | 60 mL |
| Tomato slices | 4 | 4 |
| Deli turkey breast slices | 3 oz. | 85 g |

Combine dressing and pesto in small cup. Spread evenly over pita.

Arrange lettuce leaves over pesto mixture. Sprinkle with cheese. Arrange tomato slices in a row from top to bottom. Place turkey slices over tomato. Fold in sides, leaving ends open. Place, seam-side down, on plate. Makes 1 pita.

*1 pita: 443 Calories; 18.0 g Total Fat (6.9 g Mono, 3.2 g Poly, 6.8 g Sat); 60 mg Cholesterol; 44 g Carbohydrate; 3 g Fibre; 27 g Protein; 1587 mg Sodium*

Pictured on page 35.

**TURKEY WRAP:** Use a flour tortilla instead of pita bread.

# Meatza Pizza

*This manly meat masterpiece is sure to put any pizzeria to shame.*
*Ordinary pizza sauce not macho enough for you? We've used*
*barbecue sauce, a natural fit with all your favourite meats.*

| | | |
|---|---|---|
| **Prebaked pizza crust** | 1 | 1 |
| (12 inch, 30 cm, diameter) | | |
| **Barbecue sauce** | 1/3 cup | 75 mL |
| **Chopped cooked ham** | 1 cup | 250 mL |
| **Chopped cooked roast beef (see Note)** | 1 cup | 250 mL |
| **Chopped pepperoni** | 1 cup | 250 mL |
| **Grated mozzarella cheese** | 1 3/4 cups | 425 mL |

Preheat oven to 425°F (220°C). Place crust on greased 12 inch (30 cm)
pizza pan. Spread barbecue sauce evenly over crust.

Sprinkle next 3 ingredients over sauce.

Sprinkle cheese over top. Bake for about 10 minutes until heated through
and cheese is golden. Cuts into 8 wedges.

*1 wedge: 254 Calories; 16.3 g Total Fat (6.5 g Mono, 1.2 g Poly, 7.2 g Sat); 48 mg Cholesterol;*
*6 g Carbohydrate; 1 g Fibre; 19 g Protein; 537 mg Sodium*

Pictured on page 35.

**Note:** If you don't have any leftover roast beef, use deli roast beef
slices instead.

1. Meatza Pizza, above
2. Turkey Pita, page 33
3. Denver Noodle Frittata, page 32

Props courtesy of: The Bay

# Peachy-Keen Crepe

*If you're keen on crepes but a little afraid to make them, try these effort-free crepes that bake in your oven. Watch the crepe reach great heights as it bakes (it'll deflate when it's out of the oven). It's just peachy!*

| | | |
|---|---|---|
| Large eggs | 2 | 2 |
| Milk | 1/2 cup | 125 mL |
| Butter (or hard margarine), melted | 2 tbsp. | 30 mL |
| All-purpose flour | 1/2 cup | 125 mL |
| Salt | 1/4 tsp. | 1 mL |
| Can of sliced peaches in syrup, drained | 14 oz. | 398 mL |
| Maple (or maple-flavoured) syrup | 1/3 cup | 75 mL |

Preheat oven to 450°F (230°C). Place 9 x 9 inch (22 x 22 cm) pan in oven. Whisk first 3 ingredients in medium bowl.

Add flour and salt. Beat until smooth. Spray hot pan with cooking spray. Pour batter into pan. Bake for about 12 minutes until edges are browned and middle is puffed up.

Meanwhile, combine peaches and syrup in small bowl. Cut crepe into 4 equal portions. Spoon peach mixture over top. Serves 4.

*1 serving: 295 Calories; 8.7 g Total Fat (2.7 g Mono, 0.6 g Poly, 4.6 g Sat); 110 mg Cholesterol; 50 g Carbohydrate; 2 g Fibre; 6 g Protein; 241 mg Sodium*

Pictured on page 36.

1. Fresh Breakfast Salad, page 38
2. Peachy-Keen Crepe, above
3. Easy Eggs Benny, page 41

Props courtesy of: Pier 1 Imports
Stokes

# Fresh Breakfast Salad

*After a long, restful sleep, refresh yourself with this fantastic salad. Great for brunches, lunches or snacks. Don't be afraid to change it up with your favourite fruits, as long as you use the same amounts as called for in the recipe.*

| | | |
|---|---|---|
| Fresh strawberries, halved | 2 1/2 cups | 625 mL |
| Medium bananas, sliced | 2 | 2 |
| Medium peeled oranges, halved and sliced | 2 | 2 |
| Orange juice | 1/4 cup | 60 mL |
| Liquid honey | 2 tbsp. | 30 mL |
| Sliced almonds, toasted (see Coach, page 63), optional | 2 tbsp. | 30 mL |

Put first 3 ingredients into medium bowl.

Combine orange juice and honey in small bowl. Drizzle over fruit mixture. Toss gently.

Sprinkle almonds over top. Makes about 4 cups (1 L).

*1 cup (250 mL): 159 Calories; 0.6 g Total Fat (0.1 g Mono, 0.2 g Poly, 0.1 g Sat); 0 mg Cholesterol; 40 g Carbohydrate; 4 g Fibre; 2 g Protein; 2 mg Sodium*

Pictured on page 36.

# Tropical Burst

*Give yourself a burst of morning energy with this sweet, refreshing smoothie. Perfect for those grab-and-go mornings.*

| | | |
|---|---|---|
| Frozen overripe medium banana (see Coach, page 39), cut up | 1 | 1 |
| Apple juice | 1 cup | 250 mL |
| Vanilla frozen yogurt | 1/4 cup | 60 mL |
| Medium unsweetened coconut | 1 tbsp. | 15 mL |

Put all 4 ingredients into blender. Process until smooth. Makes about 1 3/4 cups (425 mL).

*1 cup (250 mL): 174 Calories; 3.2 g Total Fat (0.4 g Mono, 0.2 g Poly, 2.3 g Sat); trace Cholesterol; 37 g Carbohydrate; 2 g Fibre; 2 g Protein; 29 mg Sodium*

# Buttery Orange Scones

*Sweet, rich scones are a wonderful addition to morning coffee or tea. The simple addition of orange zest adds a subtle, yet complex, new dimension. Give your co-workers some special attention and bring these in for a morning treat.*

| | | |
|---|---|---|
| All-purpose flour | 1 3/4 cups | 425 mL |
| Granulated sugar | 1/2 cup | 125 mL |
| Baking powder | 2 tsp. | 10 mL |
| Salt | 1/2 tsp. | 2 mL |
| Cold butter (or hard margarine), cut up | 1/3 cup | 75 mL |
| Large egg, fork-beaten | 1 | 1 |
| Milk | 1/3 cup | 75 mL |
| Grated orange zest | 1 tsp. | 5 mL |
| Granulated sugar | 2 tsp. | 10 mL |

Preheat oven to 375°F (190°C). Combine first 4 ingredients in large bowl. Cut in butter until mixture resembles coarse crumbs. Make a well in centre.

Combine next 3 ingredients in small bowl. Add to well. Stir until soft dough forms. Turn out onto lightly floured surface. Knead 6 times. Pat out to 6 inch (15 cm) square, about 3/4 inch (2 cm) thick.

Sprinkle second amount of sugar over top. Cut into nine 2 x 2 inch (5 x 5 cm) squares. Arrange squares 2 inches (5 cm) apart on greased baking sheet. Bake for 15 to 20 minutes until edges are golden. Makes 9 scones.

*1 scone: 196 Calories; 7.4 g Total Fat (2.0 g Mono, 0.3 g Poly, 4.5 g Sat); 39 mg Cholesterol; 30 g Carbohydrate; trace Fibre; 3 g Protein; 247 mg Sodium*

When your bananas get too ripe to enjoy fresh, peel and cut them into 2 inch (5 cm) chunks and freeze on a baking sheet. Once frozen, transfer to a freezer bag for use in any blended beverage. Ripe bananas have superior flavour for beverages.

# Quick Quiche Squares

*A bacon and red pepper quiche can come together at quantum speeds—*
*when it's in biscuit form. Serve with salad for lunch, or toast for brunch.*

| | | |
|---|---|---|
| Chopped onion | 1/2 cup | 125 mL |
| Bacon slices, diced | 3 | 3 |
| Large eggs | 3 | 3 |
| Biscuit mix | 2/3 cup | 150 mL |
| Milk | 1/2 cup | 125 mL |
| Salt | 1/4 tsp. | 1 mL |
| Grated Swiss cheese | 1 cup | 250 mL |
| Chopped roasted red pepper | 1/2 cup | 125 mL |

Preheat oven to 400°F (205°C). Cook onion and bacon in large frying pan on medium-high for 2 to 4 minutes until bacon is browned.

Meanwhile, whisk next 4 ingredients in large bowl until smooth.

Add cheese, red pepper and bacon mixture. Stir. Pour into greased 9 x 9 inch (22 x 22 cm) baking dish. Bake for about 20 minutes until set and knife inserted in centre comes out clean. Cuts into 6 squares.

*1 square: 295 Calories; 17.9 g Total Fat (6.7 g Mono, 1.7 g Poly, 8.4 g Sat); 119 mg Cholesterol; 20 g Carbohydrate; 1 g Fibre; 12 g Protein; 604 mg Sodium*

COACH

Don't worry about roasting your own peppers—
you can get jars of them in the same aisle you'd find pickles.

# Easy Eggs Benny

*We've simplified hollandaise sauce so you can enjoy the great taste
of eggs Benedict whenever you like. This recipe can also
be made with fried eggs if you prefer not to poach them.*

| | | |
|---|---|---|
| Water, approximately | 4 cups | 1 L |
| White vinegar | 2 tsp. | 10 mL |
| Large eggs | 4 | 4 |
| Mayonnaise | 2 tbsp. | 30 mL |
| Plain yogurt | 2 tbsp. | 30 mL |
| Dijon mustard | 1/2 tsp. | 2 mL |
| Lemon juice | 1/4 tsp. | 1 mL |
| Paprika, just a pinch | | |
| Plain English muffins, split | 2 | 2 |
| Deli ham slices (about 3 oz., 85 g) | 4 | 4 |

Pour water into medium saucepan until about 1 1/2 inches (3.8 cm) deep.
Add vinegar. Stir. Bring to a boil. Reduce heat to medium. Water should
continue to simmer. Break 1 egg into shallow dish. Slip egg into water.
Repeat with remaining eggs. Cook for 2 to 3 minutes until egg whites
are set and yolks reach desired doneness. Remove eggs with slotted spoon.
Blot dry with paper towels.

Meanwhile, combine next 5 ingredients in small bowl.

Toast English muffin halves. Place 1 ham slice on each muffin half.
Place eggs over ham. Top with yogurt mixture. Serves 4.

*1 serving: 202 Calories; 9.7 g Total Fat (4.3 g Mono, 2.0 g Poly, 2.1 g Sat); 199 mg Cholesterol;
15 g Carbohydrate; 1 g Fibre; 13 g Protein; 509 mg Sodium*

Pictured on page 36.

COACH

Can't tell if your poached egg is ready? If you like your
egg yolk soft and runny, cook for about three minutes.
For a firmer yolk, cook for about four minutes.

# Blueberry Lemon Muffins

*This classic morning treat is all jazzed up with a hint of lemon.*
*Use the juice from your lemon to make soured milk for this recipe.*

| | | |
|---|---|---|
| All-purpose flour | 2 cups | 500 mL |
| Granulated sugar | 3/4 cup | 175 mL |
| Baking powder | 2 tsp. | 10 mL |
| Baking soda | 1/2 tsp. | 2 mL |
| Salt | 1/2 tsp. | 2 mL |
| Large egg, fork-beaten | 1 | 1 |
| Buttermilk (or soured milk, see Coach, below) | 1 cup | 250 mL |
| Butter (or hard margarine), melted | 1/3 cup | 75 mL |
| Grated lemon zest | 1 tsp. | 5 mL |
| Vanilla extract | 1 tsp. | 5 mL |
| Fresh (or frozen) blueberries | 1 cup | 250 mL |

Preheat oven to 400°F (205°C). Measure first 5 ingredients into large bowl. Stir. Make a well in centre.

Combine next 5 ingredients in medium bowl. Add to well.

Add blueberries. Stir until just moistened. Fill 24 mini-muffin cups 3/4 full. Bake for 12 to 14 minutes until wooden pick inserted in centre of muffin comes out clean. Let stand in pan for 5 minutes. Remove muffins from pan and place on wire rack to cool. Makes 24 mini-muffins.

*1 mini-muffin: 90 Calories; 2.8 g Total Fat (0.1 g Mono, trace Poly, 1.7 g Sat); 15 mg Cholesterol; 15 g Carbohydrate; trace Fibre; 2 g Protein; 130 mg Sodium*

**COACH** To make soured milk, measure 1 tbsp. (15 mL) white vinegar or lemon juice into a 1 cup (250 mL) liquid measure. Add enough milk to make 1 cup (250 mL). Stir. Let stand for 1 minute.

# Baked French Toast

*Do you ever wish that you could do a whole bunch of things at one time?*
*Well, this recipe helps you multi-task. You can bake your French toast while you*
*read the morning paper—no one will know you weren't slaving over a hot stove!*

| | | |
|---|---|---|
| Large eggs | 8 | 8 |
| Can of evaporated milk | 13 1/2 oz. | 385 mL |
| Granulated sugar | 1 tbsp. | 15 mL |
| Vanilla extract | 1 tsp. | 5 mL |
| Ground cinnamon | 1/2 tsp. | 2 mL |
| Butter (or hard margarine), melted | 2 tbsp. | 30 mL |
| Day-old French bread slices | 12 | 12 |
| (1 inch, 2.5 cm, thick) | | |
| Can of apple pie filling | 19 oz. | 540 mL |
| Maple (or maple-flavoured) syrup | 1/2 cup | 125 mL |
| Ground cinnamon | 1 tsp. | 5 mL |
| Icing (confectioner's) sugar | 2 tbsp. | 30 mL |

Preheat oven to 425°F (220°C). Whisk eggs in large bowl until frothy.
Add next 4 ingredients. Whisk until well combined.

Brush 10 x 15 inch (25 x 38 cm) baking sheet with sides with butter.
Dip 1 bread slice into egg mixture. Turn to coat both sides. Place on
baking sheet. Repeat with remaining bread slices and egg mixture. Pour
remaining egg mixture over top. Bake for about 15 minutes until golden.

Meanwhile, combine next 3 ingredients in medium saucepan. Heat and
stir on medium until heated through. Cover to keep warm.

Transfer toast to large serving platter. Sprinkle icing sugar over top.
Serve apple mixture on the side. Serves 4.

*1 serving: 865 Calories; 21.0 g Total Fat (7.7 g Mono, 2.6 g Poly, 8.6 g Sat); 395 mg Cholesterol;*
*140 g Carbohydrate; 5 g Fibre; 29 g Protein; 986 mg Sodium*

# Steak Salads

*A great example of how to turn a salad into a meal. If you aren't
in a rush, you can easily wash and cut your own lettuce (it's a lot cheaper).
And if you love horseradish, double the amount.*

| | | |
|---|---|---|
| Cooking oil | 1 tbsp. | 15 mL |
| Beef top sirloin steak | 3/4 lb. | 340 g |
| Seasoned salt, sprinkle | | |
| Iceberg lettuce mix, lightly packed | 8 cups | 2 L |
| Snow peas, trimmed and halved | 1 cup | 250 mL |
| Grated medium Cheddar cheese | 1/2 cup | 125 mL |
| Thinly sliced green onion | 1/4 cup | 60 mL |
| Coleslaw dressing | 1/3 cup | 75 mL |
| Prepared horseradish | 1 tsp. | 5 mL |

Heat cooking oil in large frying pan on medium-high. Sprinkle both sides
of steak with seasoned salt. Add to frying pan. Cook for about 3 minutes
per side until desired doneness. Transfer to cutting board. Let stand for
10 minutes. Cut into short, thin strips.

Meanwhile, put next 4 ingredients into large bowl.

Combine dressing and horseradish in small cup. Drizzle over lettuce
mixture. Toss. Arrange on 4 salad plates. Arrange steak over top.
Makes 4 salads.

*1 salad: 323 Calories; 20.4 g Total Fat (5.8 g Mono, 1.5 g Poly, 6.6 g Sat); 67 mg Cholesterol;
10 g Carbohydrate; 1 g Fibre; 24 g Protein; 294 mg Sodium*

# Artichoke Rotini Salad

*The addition of artichokes to this pasta salad makes it* **trés** *chic.*
*The unique spirals of rotini pasta are great for gripping creamy sauces.*

| | | |
|---|---|---|
| Water | 6 cups | 1.5 L |
| Salt | 3/4 tsp. | 4 mL |
| Rotini pasta | 2 cups | 500 mL |
| Jar of marinated artichoke hearts, drained and liquid reserved, chopped | 6 oz. | 170 mL |
| Chopped celery | 1/2 cup | 125 mL |
| Chopped green onion | 1/3 cup | 75 mL |
| Roasted red peppers, blotted dry and chopped | 1/4 cup | 60 mL |
| Mayonnaise | 1/2 cup | 125 mL |
| Reserved liquid from artichoke hearts | 1/4 cup | 60 mL |

Combine water and salt in large saucepan or Dutch oven. Bring to a boil.
Add pasta. Boil, uncovered, for about 10 minutes, stirring occasionally,
until tender but firm. Drain. Rinse with cold water. Drain well.
Transfer to large bowl.

Add next 4 ingredients. Toss.

Combine mayonnaise and reserved marinade in small bowl. Add to pasta
mixture. Toss until coated. Makes about 3 1/2 cups (875 mL).

*1 cup (250 mL): 675 Calories; 18.5 g Total Fat (9.1 g Mono, 5.5 g Poly, 1.7 g Sat); 9 mg Cholesterol;*
*108 g Carbohydrate; 6 g Fibre; 20 g Protein; 434 mg Sodium*

# Thai Chicken Salad

*This salad's sure to be the "mein" attraction on your dinner table! Crunchy chow mein noodles crown chicken and fresh greens coated in a dressing of cilantro, peanut, ginger and soy. And for an extra neat treat, try the dressing on pasta.*

### THAI DRESSING

| | | |
|---|---|---|
| Mayonnaise | 1/2 cup | 125 mL |
| Chopped fresh cilantro or parsley, lightly packed | 1/4 cup | 60 mL |
| Peanut butter | 1 tbsp. | 15 mL |
| Rice vinegar | 1 tbsp. | 15 mL |
| Soy sauce | 1 tbsp. | 15 mL |
| Garlic cloves (or 1/2 tsp., 2 mL, powder) | 2 | 2 |
| Finely grated gingerroot | 1 tsp. | 5 mL |
| Granulated sugar | 1 tsp. | 5 mL |
| Dried crushed chilies | 1/2 tsp. | 2 mL |

### SALAD

| | | |
|---|---|---|
| Cut or torn romaine lettuce, lightly packed | 6 cups | 1.5 L |
| Chopped cooked chicken (see Coach, page 31) | 4 cups | 1 L |
| Dry chow mein noodles | 1 cup | 250 mL |
| Fresh bean sprouts | 1 cup | 250 mL |
| Grated carrot | 1 cup | 250 mL |
| Thinly sliced radish (optional) | 1 cup | 250 mL |

**Thai Dressing:** Put all 9 ingredients into blender. Process for about 30 seconds until smooth. Makes about 3/4 cup (175 mL) dressing.

**Salad:** Put all 6 ingredients into large bowl. Drizzle with Thai Dressing. Toss. Makes about 10 cups (2.5 L).

*1 cup (250 mL): 236 Calories; 13.3 g Total Fat (5.8 g Mono, 4.2 g Poly, 2.2 g Sat); 56 mg Cholesterol; 10 g Carbohydrate; 2 g Fibre; 19 g Protein; 235 mg Sodium*

Pictured on page 53.

# BLT Salad

*A meal salad that tastes just like a BLT sandwich. If you'd like a little more protein, add some chopped cooked chicken, beans or a chopped hard-cooked egg.*

| | | |
|---|---|---|
| Bacon slices, diced | 12 | 12 |
| Iceberg lettuce mix, lightly packed | 8 cups | 2 L |
| Coarsely chopped tomato | 2 cups | 500 mL |
| Seasoned croutons | 1 1/2 cups | 375 mL |
| DRESSING | | |
| Salad dressing (or mayonnaise) | 1/2 cup | 125 mL |
| Milk | 3 tbsp. | 50 mL |
| Granulated sugar | 1/2 tsp. | 2 mL |
| Prepared mustard | 1/2 tsp. | 2 mL |

Cook bacon in large frying pan on medium for 8 to 10 minutes until browned. Transfer with slotted spoon to paper towel-lined plate to drain. Cool.

Meanwhile, put next 3 ingredients into large bowl.

**Dressing:** Combine all 4 ingredients in small bowl. Add to lettuce mixture. Add bacon. Toss. Makes about 12 cups (3 L).

*1 cup (250 mL): 111 Calories; 8.2 g Total Fat (4.3 g Mono, 2.1 g Poly, 1.5 g Sat); 9 mg Cholesterol; 6 g Carbohydrate; 1 g Fibre; 3 g Protein; 246 mg Sodium*

# Dill Pickle Potato Salad

*This can be your signature dish for all your family get-togethers.*
*The dill flavour makes it out of the ordinary.*

| | | |
|---|---|---|
| Baby potatoes, quartered | 1 lb. | 454 g |
| Diced dill pickle | 1/2 cup | 125 mL |
| Salad dressing (or mayonnaise) | 1/2 cup | 125 mL |
| Green onion, thinly sliced | 1 | 1 |
| Dill pickle juice | 1 tbsp. | 15 mL |
| Prepared mustard | 1 tsp. | 5 mL |
| Large hard-cooked eggs (see Coach, below), chopped | 2 | 2 |

Paprika, sprinkle

Pour water into large saucepan until about 1 inch (2.5 cm) deep. Add potatoes. Cover. Bring to a boil. Reduce heat to medium. Boil gently for 12 to 15 minutes until tender. Drain. Rinse with cold water until cooled. Drain well. Transfer to large bowl.

Combine next 5 ingredients in small bowl. Add egg. Stir. Add to potatoes. Stir until coated.

Sprinkle with paprika. Makes about 3 cups (750 mL).

*1 cup (250 mL): 375 Calories; 22.6 g Total Fat (12.1 g Mono, 6.9 g Poly, 2.4 g Sat);*
*134 mg Cholesterol; 34 g Carbohydrate; 2 g Fibre; 8 g Protein; 717 mg Sodium*

COACH

To make hard-cooked eggs, place eggs in a single layer in a saucepan. Add cold water until it's about 1 inch (2.5 cm) above the eggs. Cover. Bring to a boil. Reduce heat to medium-low. Simmer for 10 minutes. Drain. Cover the eggs with cold water. Change the water each time it warms until the eggs are cool enough to handle. Remove the shells. You can do this while the potatoes are cooking to save time.

Salads & Soups

# Taco Salad

*Honestly, do you know anyone who doesn't like taco salad?*
*It's a smart pick when you're pressed to create a crowd-pleasing dinner.*
*You can always omit the onion and garlic if time is of the essence.*

| | | |
|---|---|---|
| Cooking oil | 1 tsp. | 5 mL |
| Lean ground beef | 1 lb. | 454 g |
| Finely chopped onion | 1 cup | 250 mL |
| Garlic cloves, minced | 2 | 2 |
| (or 1/2 tsp., 2 mL, powder) | | |
| Envelope of taco seasoning mix | 1 1/4 oz. | 35 g |
| Iceberg lettuce mix, lightly packed | 8 cups | 2 L |
| Grated Mexican cheese blend | 2 cups | 500 mL |
| Chopped tomato | 1 cup | 250 mL |
| Frozen kernel corn, thawed | 1 cup | 250 mL |
| Can of sliced black olives, drained | 4 1/2 oz. | 125 mL |
| Ranch (or Thousand Island) dressing | 1 cup | 250 mL |
| Tortilla chips | 4 cups | 1 L |

Heat cooking oil in large frying pan on medium. Add next 3 ingredients. Scramble-fry for about 10 minutes until beef is no longer pink. Drain.

Add taco seasoning. Heat and stir for 1 minute. Transfer to baking sheet with sides. Spread in thin layer. Chill until cool.

Meanwhile, put next 5 ingredients into large bowl. Toss. Add beef.

Drizzle with dressing. Toss.

Serve with tortilla chips. Serves 4.

*1 serving: 1020 Calories; 69.7 g Total Fat (8.7 g Mono, 2.7 g Poly, 22.8 g Sat); 155 mg Cholesterol; 44 g Carbohydrate; 4 g Fibre; 52 g Protein; 2298 mg Sodium*

COACH

For a fancier presentation, ingredients can be layered in a clear bowl and tossed at the table before serving. Or consider "plating" the salads. This means you make individual salads for everyone, rather than one big one.

# Lentil Feta Salad

*Although they're teeny tiny, lentils pack a hearty punch and make this salad quite filling.*

| | | |
|---|---|---|
| Can of lentils, rinsed and drained | 19 oz. | 540 mL |
| Chopped green pepper | 1/2 cup | 125 mL |
| Chopped red pepper | 1/2 cup | 125 mL |
| Chopped tomato | 1/2 cup | 125 mL |
| Chopped green onion | 1/4 cup | 60 mL |
| Italian dressing | 1/4 cup | 60 mL |
| Lemon juice | 2 tbsp. | 30 mL |
| Granulated sugar | 1 tsp. | 5 mL |
| Pepper | 1/4 tsp. | 1 mL |
| Crumbled feta cheese | 1 cup | 250 mL |

Combine first 5 ingredients in medium bowl.

Combine next 4 ingredients in small cup. Drizzle over lentil mixture. Toss until coated.

Sprinkle with feta cheese. Makes about 4 1/2 cups (1.1 L).

*1 cup (250 mL): 282 Calories; 16.5 g Total Fat (6.6 g Mono, 3.3 g Poly, 5.8 g Sat); 39 mg Cholesterol; 22 g Carbohydrate; 9 g Fibre; 13 g Protein; 730 mg Sodium*

Pictured on page 143.

# Hot-And-Sour Slaw

*Be the hot topic at the next potluck with this uniquely spicy slaw.*

| | | |
|---|---|---|
| Coleslaw mix | 8 cups | 2 L |
| Can of sliced water chestnuts, drained and chopped | 8 oz. | 227 mL |
| Thinly sliced red onion | 1/2 cup | 125 mL |
| HOT-AND-SOUR DRESSING | | |
| Rice vinegar | 1/4 cup | 60 mL |
| Lime juice | 2 tbsp. | 30 mL |
| Soy sauce | 2 tbsp. | 30 mL |
| Granulated sugar | 1 tbsp. | 15 mL |

*(continued on next page)*

Salads & Soups

| | | |
|---|---|---|
| Garlic clove, minced (or 1/4 tsp., 1 mL, powder) | 1 | 1 |
| Dried crushed chilies | 1/4 tsp. | 1 mL |

Put first 3 ingredients into large bowl. Toss.

**Hot-And-Sour Dressing:** Combine all 6 ingredients in jar with tight-fitting lid. Shake well. Makes about 1/2 cup (125 mL) dressing. Drizzle over salad. Toss. Makes about 8 cups (2 L).

*1 cup (250 mL): 55 Calories; 0.3 g Total Fat (trace Mono, 0.1 g Poly, trace Sat); 0 mg Cholesterol; 13 g Carbohydrate; 4 g Fibre; 2 g Protein; 233 mg Sodium*

---

# Spinach Pesto Salad

*The bold basil-scented vinaigrette adds a refreshing flair
to this spinach salad loaded with pine nuts and sweet tomatoes.*

**PESTO VINAIGRETTE**

| | | |
|---|---|---|
| Basil pesto | 3 tbsp. | 50 mL |
| Apple cider vinegar | 2 tbsp. | 30 mL |
| Olive (or cooking) oil | 2 tbsp. | 30 mL |
| Grated lemon zest | 1 tsp. | 5 mL |
| Salt | 1/8 tsp. | 0.5 mL |

**SALAD**

| | | |
|---|---|---|
| Fresh spinach leaves, lightly packed | 6 cups | 1.5 L |
| Grape tomatoes | 1 cup | 250 mL |
| Pine nuts, toasted (see Coach, page 63) | 2/3 cup | 150 mL |

**Pesto Vinaigrette:** Combine all 5 ingredients in jar with tight-fitting lid. Shake well. Makes about 1/2 cup (125 mL) vinaigrette.

**Salad:** Put all 3 ingredients into large bowl. Drizzle with Pesto Vinaigrette. Toss. Makes about 6 cups (1.5 L).

*1 cup (250 mL): 179 Calories; 16.2 g Total Fat (7.4 g Mono, 5.3 g Poly, 2.4 g Sat); trace Cholesterol; 6 g Carbohydrate; 4 g Fibre; 6 g Protein; 159 mg Sodium*

Pictured on page 53.

# Chicken Salad Fiesta

*A bean salad with a spicy zing. If you want to up the crunch factor,*
*serve on a bed of crisp lettuce.*

| | | |
|---|---|---|
| Chopped cooked chicken (see Coach, page 31) | 3 cups | 750 mL |
| Canned black beans, rinsed and drained | 1 cup | 250 mL |
| Frozen kernel corn, thawed | 1 cup | 250 mL |
| Chopped red pepper | 1/2 cup | 125 mL |
| Grated lime zest | 1 tsp. | 5 mL |
| Salsa | 1 cup | 250 mL |
| Ketchup | 1 tbsp. | 15 mL |
| Lime juice | 1 tbsp. | 15 mL |
| Olive (or cooking) oil | 1 tbsp. | 15 mL |
| Garlic clove, minced (or 1/4 tsp., 1 mL, powder) | 1 | 1 |
| Salt | 1/4 tsp. | 1 mL |
| Drops of hot pepper sauce | 4 | 4 |

Chopped fresh parsley, for garnish

Combine first 5 ingredients in large bowl.

Combine next 7 ingredients in small bowl. Add to chicken mixture.
Toss until coated.

Sprinkle with parsley. Makes about 5 cups (1.25 L).

*1 cup (250 mL): 284 Calories; 10.7 g Total Fat (4.8 g Mono, 2.1 g Poly, 2.5 g Sat);*
*79 mg Cholesterol; 19 g Carbohydrate; 4 g Fibre; 29 g Protein; 667 mg Sodium*

1. Spinach Pesto Salad, page 51
2. Thai Chicken Salad, page 46
3. White Bean Soup, page 56

Props courtesy of: Casa Bugatti
Pier 1 Imports
Stokes

# Simple Salad

*Sometimes you just want a good ol' green salad. The vinaigrette makes it special.*

| | | |
|---|---|---|
| Mixed salad greens, lightly packed | 8 cups | 2 L |
| Sliced red pepper | 1 1/2 cups | 375 mL |
| Chopped walnuts, toasted | 1/3 cup | 75 mL |
| (see Coach, page 63) | | |
| Raisins | 1/3 cup | 75 mL |
| Sliced red onion | 1/4 cup | 60 mL |
| SIMPLE DRESSING | | |
| Olive (or cooking) oil | 1/4 cup | 60 mL |
| White vinegar | 2 tbsp. | 30 mL |
| Granulated sugar | 2 tsp. | 10 mL |
| Dry mustard | 1/2 tsp. | 2 mL |
| Salt | 1/8 tsp. | 0.5 mL |

Put first 5 ingredients into large bowl. Toss.

**Simple Dressing:** Combine all 5 ingredients in jar with tight-fitting lid. Shake well. Makes about 1/3 cup (75 mL) dressing. Drizzle over lettuce mixture. Toss until coated. Makes about 9 cups (2.25 L).

*1 cup (250 mL): 121 Calories; 9.1 g Total Fat (4.8 g Mono, 2.7 g Poly, 1.1 g Sat); 0 mg Cholesterol; 10 g Carbohydrate; 2 g Fibre; 2 g Protein; 53 mg Sodium*

Pictured on page 54.

1. Italian Garlic Bread, page 76
2. Simple Salad, above
3. Chicken Picadillo, page 102

Props courtesy of: Pier 1 Imports
Danesco Inc.

# White Bean Soup

*Feel like you've "bean there, done that?" Try this bean soup with a difference.*
*The fresh flavours of green onion and tomato are showcased in this spicy purée.*
*Use double the amount of chilies if you love spicy food.*

| | | |
|---|---|---|
| Bacon slices, diced | 4 | 4 |
| Chopped onion | 1 cup | 250 mL |
| Sliced celery | 3/4 cup | 175 mL |
| Bay leaf | 1 | 1 |
| Dried crushed chilies | 1/4 tsp. | 1 mL |
| Pepper | 1/4 tsp. | 1 mL |
| Prepared chicken broth | 4 cups | 1 L |
| Can of navy (or white kidney) beans, rinsed and drained | 19 oz. | 540 mL |
| Finely chopped Roma (plum) tomato | 3/4 cup | 175 mL |
| Chopped green onion | 2 tbsp. | 30 mL |

Cook bacon in large saucepan on medium-high until crisp. Transfer with slotted spoon to paper towel-lined plate to drain.

Heat 1 tbsp. (15 mL) drippings in same saucepan on medium. Add next 5 ingredients. Cook, uncovered, for about 5 minutes, stirring often (see Note), until onion is softened.

Add broth and beans. Bring to a boil. Reduce heat to medium. Boil gently, uncovered, for 5 minutes to blend flavours. Remove from heat. Discard bay leaf. Carefully process with hand blender or in blender until smooth.

Add tomato, green onion and bacon. Stir. Makes about 6 cups (1.5 L).

*1 cup (250 mL): 169 Calories; 4.4 g Total Fat (1.9 g Mono, 0.8 g Poly, 1.4 g Sat); 6 mg Cholesterol; 24 g Carbohydrate; 6 g Fibre; 10 g Protein; 1500 mg Sodium*

Pictured on page 53.

**Note:** While stirring, be careful not to break up the bay leaf.

To make this soup even faster, use 2 tbsp. (30 mL) bacon bits and 1 tbsp. (15 mL) cooking oil instead of bacon and drippings.

**56**     Salads & Soups

# Dill-icious Spring Soup

*Enjoy the colours and flavours of spring any time of year. If you process the hot soup in your blender, be sure to hold a tea towel over the lid while blending.*

| | | |
|---|---|---|
| Butter (or hard margarine) | 2 tbsp. | 30 mL |
| Finely chopped onion | 1/2 cup | 125 mL |
| Garlic clove, minced | 1 | 1 |
| (or 1/4 tsp., 1 mL, powder) | | |
| All-purpose flour | 2 tbsp. | 30 mL |
| Prepared chicken broth | 3 cups | 750 mL |
| Chopped fresh asparagus | 1 1/2 cups | 375 mL |
| Frozen peas | 1 cup | 250 mL |
| Grated lemon zest | 2 tsp. | 10 mL |
| Bay leaf | 1 | 1 |
| Seasoned salt | 1/2 tsp. | 2 mL |
| Half-and-half cream | 1/2 cup | 125 mL |
| Chopped fresh dill (or 1 tbsp., 15 mL, dried) | 1/4 cup | 60 mL |

Melt butter in large saucepan on medium-high. Add onion and garlic. Cook for about 2 minutes, stirring often, until onion is softened.

Sprinkle with flour. Heat and stir for 1 minute.

Slowly add 1 cup (250 mL) broth. Heat and stir until boiling and thickened. Add remaining broth and next 5 ingredients. Stir. Reduce heat to medium-low. Simmer, covered, for about 5 minutes, stirring occasionally, until asparagus is tender. Discard bay leaf.

Add cream and dill. Cook and stir for about 1 minute until heated through. Carefully process with hand blender or in blender until smooth. Makes about 5 cups (1.25 L).

*1 cup (250 mL): 201 Calories; 8.2 g Total Fat (2.3 g Mono, 0.6 g Poly, 4.9 g Sat); 21 mg Cholesterol; 22 g Carbohydrate; 8 g Fibre; 10 g Protein; 1105 mg Sodium*

Soups that don't have pasta or potatoes in them are great for freezing. Make double the batch and freeze in individual containers for lunches. If the soup has milk or cream in it, expect it to separate after freezing. Just whisk it up while heating and it will be as good as new.

# Ginger Carrot Soup

*Think carrot soup is rabbit feed? No way! This vibrant,*
*smooth soup packs one heck of a gingery punch.*

| | | |
|---|---|---|
| Cooking oil | 1/2 tsp. | 2 mL |
| Frozen sliced carrots | 4 cups | 1 L |
| Chopped onion | 1 cup | 250 mL |
| Finely grated gingerroot | 1 tsp. | 5 mL |
| (or 1/4 tsp., 1 mL, ground ginger) | | |
| Prepared chicken broth | 4 cups | 1 L |
| Curry powder | 1/4 tsp. | 1 mL |
| Garlic powder | 1/4 tsp. | 1 mL |
| Salt | 1/2 tsp. | 2 mL |
| Pepper | 1/8 tsp. | 0.5 mL |
| Evaporated milk (or half-and-half cream) | 1 cup | 250 mL |

Heat cooking oil in large saucepan on medium-high. Add carrot and onion. Cook for about 5 minutes, stirring often, until onion starts to soften.

Add ginger. Stir.

Add next 5 ingredients. Stir. Bring to a boil. Reduce heat to medium. Boil gently, covered, for about 15 minutes until carrot is tender. Remove from heat.

Add evaporated milk. Stir. Carefully process with hand blender or in blender until smooth. Makes about 8 cups (2 L) of super soup for you and your lucky friends.

*1 cup (250 mL): 77 Calories; 1.6 g Total Fat (0.6 g Mono, 0.4 g Poly, 0.6 g Sat); 2 mg Cholesterol; 12 g Carbohydrate; 2 g Fibre; 4 g Protein; 961 mg Sodium*

COACH

Lots of people peel gingerroot with a vegetable peeler— this works but it does create a lot of waste. Because the skin on the ginger is so thin, you can actually peel it off by scraping it with the edge of a spoon—it comes off very easily.

# Quick Tomato Soup

*Consider this your most basic soup recipe.*

| | | |
|---|---|---|
| Cooking oil | 1 tsp. | 5 mL |
| Chopped onion | 1 cup | 250 mL |
| Can of diced tomatoes (with juice) | 28 oz. | 796 mL |
| Prepared chicken (or vegetable) broth | 2 cups | 500 mL |
| Can of tomato sauce | 7 1/2 oz. | 213 mL |
| Whipping cream | 1/2 cup | 125 mL |
| Chopped fresh basil | 2 tbsp. | 30 mL |

Heat cooking oil in large saucepan on medium. Add onion. Cook, uncovered, for 5 to 10 minutes, stirring often, until softened.

Add next 3 ingredients. Stir. Bring to a boil. Reduce heat to medium-low. Simmer, partially covered, for 5 minutes to blend flavours.

Add cream and basil. Stir. Carefully process with hand blender or in blender until smooth. Makes about 6 cups (1.5 L).

*1 cup (250 mL): 123 Calories; 8.2 g Total Fat (2.6 g Mono, 0.6 g Poly, 4.5 g Sat); 25 mg Cholesterol; 12 g Carbohydrate; 1 g Fibre; 3 g Protein; 1078 mg Sodium*

# Spicy Gazpacho

*This chilled soup is quick, spicy, healthy and brilliantly coloured.*

| | | |
|---|---|---|
| Tomato juice | 2 cups | 500 mL |
| Finely chopped English cucumber (with peel) | 1 cup | 250 mL |
| Finely chopped Roma (plum) tomato | 1 cup | 250 mL |
| Finely chopped onion | 1/2 cup | 125 mL |
| Finely chopped yellow pepper | 1/2 cup | 125 mL |
| Lime juice | 2 tbsp. | 30 mL |
| Granulated sugar | 2 tsp. | 10 mL |
| Chili paste (sambal oelek) | 1 tsp. | 5 mL |
| Salt | 1/2 tsp. | 2 mL |
| Pepper | 1/2 tsp. | 2 mL |

Combine all 10 ingredients in large bowl. Ladle half of vegetable mixture into blender. Process until almost smooth. Return to same bowl. Stir. Makes about 4 cups (1 L).

*1 cup (250 mL): 59 Calories; 0.3 g Total Fat (0.1 g Mono, 0.1 g Poly, 0.1 g Sat); 0 mg Cholesterol; 14 g Carbohydrate; 2 g Fibre; 2 g Protein; 763 mg Sodium*

# Spicy Potato Wedges

*Live life on the wedge! These spicy fries are a great alternative to deep-fried potatoes—they're less messy and more healthy to boot.*

| | | |
|---|---|---|
| Large unpeeled potatoes | 2 | 2 |
| Cooking oil | 1 tbsp. | 15 mL |
| Montreal steak spice | 1 tbsp. | 15 mL |

Preheat oven to 425°F (220°C). Prick potatoes in several places with fork. Wrap individually with paper towel. Microwave on high (100%) for 8 to 10 minutes, turning at halftime, until tender. Let stand for about 3 minutes until cool enough to handle. Cut potatoes lengthwise into 8 wedges each. Transfer to medium bowl.

Add cooking oil. Toss until coated. Arrange wedges on greased baking sheet with sides.

Sprinkle steak spice over top. Bake for about 10 minutes until heated through. Makes 16 wedges.

*1 wedge: 43 Calories; 0.9 g Total Fat (0.5 g Mono, 0.3 g Poly, 0.1 g Sat); 0 mg Cholesterol; 8 g Carbohydrate; 1 g Fibre; 1 g Protein; 95 mg Sodium*

# Sun-Dried Tomato Asparagus

*Even though it's a vegetable, many people think asparagus is a real treat— especially when it's dressed up with tangy balsamic vinegar and flavourful pesto.*

| | | |
|---|---|---|
| Fresh asparagus, trimmed of tough ends | 1 lb. | 454 g |
| Salt | 1/2 tsp. | 2 mL |
| Balsamic vinegar | 2 tbsp. | 30 mL |
| Olive (or cooking) oil | 1 tbsp. | 15 mL |
| Sun-dried tomato pesto | 1 tbsp. | 15 mL |
| Grated lemon zest | 1/2 tsp. | 2 mL |
| Grated Parmesan cheese | 2 tbsp. | 30 mL |

Pour water into large frying pan until about 1 inch (2.5 cm) deep. Add asparagus and salt. Bring to a boil. Reduce heat to medium. Boil gently for about 4 minutes until tender-crisp. Drain. Transfer to serving plate.

Meanwhile, combine next 4 ingredients in small cup. Drizzle over asparagus.

*(continued on next page)*

Sprinkle cheese over top. Serves 4.

*1 serving: 137 Calories; 7.9 g Total Fat (3.9 g Mono, 0.4 g Poly, 3.4 g Sat); 12 mg Cholesterol; 7 g Carbohydrate; 3 g Fibre; 9 g Protein; 324 mg Sodium*

To trim asparagus ends, just use kitchen scissors and snip at the point where the stalk starts to become pliable.

# Snap-To-Attention Peas And Carrots

*Get snap pea happy! This more elegant version of peas and carrots has a buttery, seasoned coating.*

| | | |
|---|---|---|
| Butter (or hard margarine) | 3 tbsp. | 50 mL |
| Sugar snap peas, trimmed | 4 cups | 1 L |
| Thinly sliced carrot | 1 cup | 250 mL |
| Dijon mustard | 2 tsp. | 10 mL |
| Balsamic vinegar | 1 tsp. | 5 mL |
| Lemon pepper | 1 tsp. | 5 mL |
| Liquid honey | 1 tsp. | 5 mL |

Melt butter in large frying pan on medium. Add peas and carrot. Stir-fry for 3 to 5 minutes until vegetables are tender-crisp.

Combine remaining 4 ingredients in small cup. Add to vegetable mixture. Toss until coated. Makes about 4 cups (1 L).

*1 cup (250 mL): 142 Calories; 8.6 g Total Fat (2.2 g Mono, 0.4 g Poly, 5.4 g Sat); 23 mg Cholesterol; 13 g Carbohydrate; 4 g Fibre; 3 g Protein; 195 mg Sodium*

Invest in a pair of kitchen scissors to make quick work of trimming the ends of sugar snap peas, and cutting all manner of things. They come in super handy. Wash them by hand or just put them in the dishwasher.

# Half-Baked,
# Completely-Good Potatoes

*Baby potatoes are all grown-up with a dusting of oregano and Parmesan.*
*These are a great match with an oven-roasted main dish. If you can't get baby*
*potatoes, just cut four large baking potatoes into eighths.*

| | | |
|---|---|---|
| Baby potatoes, larger ones cut in half | 2 lbs. | 900 g |
| Olive (or cooking) oil | 2 tbsp. | 30 mL |
| Grated Parmesan cheese | 1/4 cup | 60 mL |
| Dried oregano | 1 tsp. | 5 mL |
| Seasoned salt | 1/2 tsp. | 2 mL |
| Pepper | 1/4 tsp. | 1 mL |

Preheat oven to 450°F (230°C). Put potatoes into large microwave-safe
bowl. Microwave, covered, on high (100%) for about 8 minutes until
almost tender. Drizzle with olive oil. Toss until coated.

Meanwhile, combine remaining 4 ingredients in small bowl. Add to
potatoes. Toss until coated. Transfer to greased baking sheet with sides.
Spread evenly. Bake for about 10 minutes until potatoes are tender.
Makes about 5 cups (1.25 L).

*1 cup (250 mL): 309 Calories; 12.7 g Total Fat (6.3 g Mono, 0.6 g Poly, 5.4 g Sat);*
*19 mg Cholesterol; 33 g Carbohydrate; 2 g Fibre; 14 g Protein; 603 mg Sodium*

# Sesame Baby Bok Choy

*There's no need to be a microwave snob when you can make great dishes like this unique, Asian-flavoured bok choy side. The microwave is the busy chef's best friend. Veggies are great cooked in the microwave—they retain their color and, as long as they're not overcooked, their crispness.*

| | | |
|---|---|---|
| Whole baby bok choy, halved | 4 | 4 |
| Prepared chicken (or vegetable) broth | 1/4 cup | 60 mL |
| Hoisin sauce | 1 tbsp. | 15 mL |
| Cooking oil | 1 tsp. | 5 mL |
| Sweet chili sauce | 1 tsp. | 5 mL |
| Finely grated gingerroot | 1/2 tsp. | 2 mL |
| (or 1/8 tsp., 0.5 mL, ground ginger) | | |
| Sesame seeds, toasted (see Coach, below) | 2 tsp. | 10 mL |

Arrange bok choy in circle on large microwave-safe plate, with leaf ends toward centre of plate.

Combine next 5 ingredients in small cup. Pour over bok choy. Microwave, covered, on high (100%) for about 5 minutes until tender-crisp. Let stand, covered, for 30 seconds.

Sprinkle sesame seeds over top. Serves 4.

*1 serving: 43 Calories; 2.3 g Total Fat (1.0 g Mono, 0.9 g Poly, 0.3 g Sat); trace Cholesterol; 5 g Carbohydrate; 1 g Fibre; 2 g Protein; 224 mg Sodium*

When toasting nuts, seeds or coconut, cooking times will vary for each type of nut—so never toast them together. For small amounts, place ingredient in an ungreased shallow frying pan. Heat on medium for 3 to 5 minutes, stirring often, until golden. For larger amounts, spread ingredient evenly in an ungreased shallow pan. Bake in a 350°F (175°C) oven for 5 to 10 minutes, stirring or shaking often, until golden.

# Curry Their Favour Rice

*A curry side will spice up any main dish. The bright green peas and crunchy toasted almonds make this side a wonderful complement to grilled meats.*

| | | |
|---|---|---|
| Cooking oil | 1 tbsp. | 15 mL |
| Finely chopped onion | 1/2 cup | 125 mL |
| Grated peeled cooking apple (such as McIntosh) | 1/2 cup | 125 mL |
| Curry powder | 1 tsp. | 5 mL |
| Ground nutmeg, sprinkle | | |
| Prepared chicken broth | 2 cups | 500 mL |
| Long grain white rice | 1 cup | 250 mL |
| Frozen peas | 1/2 cup | 125 mL |
| Sliced almonds, toasted (see Coach, page 63) | 1/4 cup | 60 mL |

Heat cooking oil in medium saucepan on medium-high. Add next 4 ingredients. Cook for 2 to 4 minutes, stirring often, until onion is softened.

Add broth. Stir. Bring to a boil. Reduce heat to medium-low. Add rice. Stir. Simmer, covered, for 15 minutes, without stirring.

Add peas. Stir. Simmer, covered, for about 5 minutes, without stirring, until liquid is absorbed and rice is tender. Fluff with fork.

Sprinkle almonds over top. Makes about 3 1/2 cups (875 mL).

*1 cup (250 mL): 390 Calories; 13.5 g Total Fat (8.1 g Mono, 3.3 g Poly, 1.4 g Sat); 0 mg Cholesterol; 58 g Carbohydrate; 2 g Fibre; 10 g Protein; 875 mg Sodium*

# Glazed Dill Carrots

*Here's an easy way to make a simple side impressive.*

| | | |
|---|---|---|
| Baby carrots, halved crosswise | 3 cups | 750 mL |
| Liquid honey | 1/4 cup | 60 mL |
| Butter (or hard margarine) | 2 tbsp. | 30 mL |
| Dried dillweed | 1/2 tsp. | 2 mL |

*(continued on next page)*

Pour water into large saucepan until about 1 inch (2.5 cm) deep. Add carrots. Cover. Bring to a boil. Reduce heat to medium. Boil gently for 8 to 10 minutes until carrots are tender-crisp. Drain.

Add remaining 3 ingredients. Heat and stir until butter is melted and carrots are coated. Makes about 3 cups (750 mL).

*1 cup (250 mL): 245 Calories; 8.8 g Total Fat (2.0 g Mono, 0.9 g Poly, 5.0 g Sat); 20 mg Cholesterol; 42 g Carbohydrate; 4 g Fibre; 2 g Protein; 135 mg Sodium*

Don't overcook your dillweed—it loses more flavour the longer it's cooked.

# Champ

*This Irish-inspired spin on mashed potatoes is so simple, yet so good!*

| Cubed peeled potato | 6 cups | 1.5 L |
|---|---|---|
| Hot milk | 1 cup | 250 mL |
| Green onions, chopped | 6 | 6 |
| Butter (or hard margarine) | 1/4 cup | 60 mL |
| Salt | 1 tsp. | 5 mL |
| Pepper | 1/2 tsp. | 2 mL |

Pour water into medium saucepan until about 1 inch (2.5 cm) deep. Add potato. Cover. Bring to a boil. Reduce heat to medium. Boil gently for 12 to 15 minutes until tender. Drain. Mash.

Add remaining 5 ingredients. Mash. Makes about 6 cups (1.5 L)—enough to satisfy all the potato lovers you know.

*1 cup (250 mL): 228 Calories; 8.2 g Total Fat (2.1 g Mono, 0.4 g Poly, 5.1 g Sat); 23 mg Cholesterol; 35 g Carbohydrate; 3 g Fibre; 5 g Protein; 477 mg Sodium*

**BAKED POTATO CHAMP:** Use 1 cup (250 mL) hot sour cream and 3 tbsp. (50 mL) chopped fresh chives instead of milk and green onion. Add 3 tbsp. (50 mL) bacon bits.

**SOUTHWESTERN CHAMP:** Use 1 cup (250 mL) hot buttermilk instead of milk and butter. Omit green onion. Add 1/4 cup (60 mL) salsa, 1 tbsp. (15 mL) minced chipotle pepper in adobo sauce and 1 minced garlic clove (or 1/4 tsp., 1 mL, powder).

Beef

# Sweet Potato Couscous

*This curried couscous with tender sweet potatoes and crunchy almonds makes a perfect side for grilled meats. This dish is designed to be served warm, but if you like it hot (some do, we hear), then heat it in the microwave until the sweet potato is hot.*

| | | |
|---|---|---|
| Prepared vegetable broth | 1 1/4 cups | 300 mL |
| Butter (or hard margarine) | 2 tbsp. | 30 mL |
| Honey | 1 tbsp. | 15 mL |
| Curry powder | 1 tsp. | 5 mL |
| Pepper | 1/4 tsp. | 1 mL |
| Couscous | 1 1/4 cups | 300 mL |
| Frozen peas | 1/2 cup | 125 mL |
| Can of sweet potatoes, drained and cut into bite-sized pieces | 19 oz. | 540 mL |
| Slivered almonds | 1/4 cup | 60 mL |
| Sliced green onion | 2 tbsp. | 30 mL |

Combine first 5 ingredients in large saucepan. Bring to a boil.

Add couscous and peas. Stir. Remove from heat. Let stand, covered, for 5 minutes. Fluff with fork.

Add remaining 3 ingredients. Stir. Makes about 6 cups (1.5 L).

*1 cup (250 mL): 321 Calories; 7.5 g Total Fat (3.0 g Mono, 1.1 g Poly, 2.7 g Sat); 10 mg Cholesterol; 56 g Carbohydrate; 5 g Fibre; 8 g Protein; 171 mg Sodium*

# Braised Red Cabbage

*This uncommon side will impress any gourmet guest with
its sweet taste, cranberry tang and vibrant colour.*

| | | |
|---|---|---|
| Butter (or hard margarine) | 2 tbsp. | 30 mL |
| Chopped red cabbage | 4 cups | 1 L |
| Chopped onion | 1 cup | 250 mL |
| Apple juice | 1/2 cup | 125 mL |
| Dried cranberries | 1/2 cup | 125 mL |
| Apple cider vinegar | 2 tbsp. | 30 mL |
| Brown sugar, packed | 2 tbsp. | 30 mL |
| Salt | 1/2 tsp. | 2 mL |
| Pepper | 1/4 tsp. | 1 mL |

Heat butter in large frying pan on medium until melted and bubbles have
disappeared. Add cabbage and onion. Cook for about 5 minutes, stirring
occasionally, until cabbage starts to soften and lighten in colour. Reduce
heat to medium-low.

Add remaining 6 ingredients. Stir. Cook, covered, for about 15 minutes
until cabbage is tender-crisp. Makes about 4 cups (1 L).

*1 cup (250 mL): 173 Calories; 5.9 g Total Fat (1.5 g Mono, 0.3 g Poly, 3.6 g Sat); 15 mg Cholesterol;
32 g Carbohydrate; 3 g Fibre; 1 g Protein; 346 mg Sodium*

Pictured on page 71.

Red cabbage can make a colourful addition to an
otherwise neutral meal but if you want its colour
to pop, there are a few things you need to keep in mind:

- Always cook it with a little bit of acidic liquid (like vinegar).
- Don't cook it in aluminum cookware.
- Don't cut it with a carbon-steel knife.

# Lemon Cranberry Couscous

*The tart taste of cranberry adds a real nice zing to anything it's in. Pair this side*
*with roast chicken or pork to get the biggest bang out of your berries.*

| | | |
|---|---|---|
| Prepared chicken broth | 3 cups | 750 mL |
| Lemon juice | 2 tbsp. | 30 mL |
| Grated lemon zest (see Coach, page 80) | 2 tsp. | 10 mL |
| Box of plain couscous | 12 oz. | 340 g |
| Dried cranberries | 2/3 cup | 150 mL |
| Olive (or cooking) oil | 2 tsp. | 10 mL |
| Chopped fresh parsley | 2 tbsp. | 30 mL |

Combine first 3 ingredients in large saucepan. Bring to a boil.

Add next 3 ingredients. Stir. Remove from heat. Let stand, covered,
for 5 minutes. Fluff with fork.

Sprinkle parsley over top. Makes about 5 3/4 cups (1.45 L).

*1 cup (250 mL): 292 Calories; 2.5 g Total Fat (1.4 g Mono, 0.5 g Poly, 0.4 g Sat); 0 mg Cholesterol;
59 g Carbohydrate; 3 g Fibre; 8 g Protein; 781 mg Sodium*

Pictured on page 71.

# Sesame Ginger Chickpeas

*Chickpeas on their own are pretty boring but their subtle taste*
*makes them a great medium to showcase more vibrant flavours.*
*Serve this Asian-inspired side with chicken or pork.*

| | | |
|---|---|---|
| Cooking oil | 1 tsp. | 5 mL |
| Chopped celery | 1 cup | 250 mL |
| Chopped onion | 1 cup | 250 mL |
| Can of chickpeas (garbanzo beans), rinsed and drained | 19 oz. | 540 mL |
| Chopped red pepper | 1 cup | 250 mL |
| Sesame ginger dressing | 1/3 cup | 75 mL |
| Chopped fresh parsley | 1 tbsp. | 15 mL |

*(continued on next page)*

Heat cooking oil in medium saucepan on medium. Add celery and onion. Cook for about 5 minutes, stirring often, until onion starts to soften.

Add next 3 ingredients. Stir. Cook, covered, for 3 to 5 minutes until heated through.

Sprinkle parsley over top. Makes about 3 1/2 cups (875 mL).

*1 cup (250 mL): 268 Calories; 11.9 g Total Fat (1.4 g Mono, 1.7 g Poly, 1.2 g Sat); 0 mg Cholesterol; 34 g Carbohydrate; 8 g Fibre; 9 g Protein; 386 mg Sodium*

---

# Bacon Garlic Green Beans

*Bacon adds a wonderful smoky flavour to almost any veggie.
If you're in a rush or just plain out of bacon, use real bacon bits instead—
just add them with the basil.*

| | | |
|---|---|---|
| Bacon slices, diced | 2 | 2 |
| Fresh (or frozen, thawed) whole green beans | 4 cups | 1 L |
| Prepared chicken broth | 1/4 cup | 60 mL |
| Garlic clove, minced | 1 | 1 |
| (or 1/4 tsp., 1 mL, powder) | | |
| Chopped fresh basil | 1 tbsp. | 15 mL |

Cook bacon in large frying pan on medium-high for about 3 minutes until starting to brown.

Add next 3 ingredients. Stir. Reduce heat to medium. Cook, covered, for 5 to 6 minutes, stirring at halftime, until green beans are tender-crisp.

Add basil. Toss. Makes about 4 cups (1 L).

*1 cup (250 mL): 115 Calories; 5.7 g Total Fat (3.6 g Mono, 1.0 g Poly, 3.1 g Sat); 8 mg Cholesterol; 14 g Carbohydrate; 5 g Fibre; 5 g Protein; 168 mg Sodium*

Recipes rarely call for a whole package of bacon, so it's wise to separate a package into smaller bundles of two or three strips each. Just wrap the bundles well in plastic wrap and put them in the freezer.

# Orange Teriyaki Stir-Fry

*Serve your nearest and dearest this citrusy stir-fry and they'll be (teri)yakkin'*
*about it for days to come. And with frozen veggies you still get all of the flavour*
*and nutrition and none of the chopping, slicing and peeling.*

| | | |
|---|---|---|
| Soy sauce | 2 tbsp. | 30 mL |
| Cornstarch | 1 tsp. | 5 mL |
| Orange juice | 1/2 cup | 125 mL |
| Brown sugar, packed | 1 tbsp. | 15 mL |
| Chili sauce | 2 tsp. | 10 mL |
| Finely grated gingerroot | 2 tsp. | 10 mL |
| (or 1/2 tsp., 2 mL, ground ginger) | | |
| Garlic cloves, minced | 2 | 2 |
| (or 1/2 tsp., 2 mL, powder) | | |
| Grated orange zest | 1 tsp. | 5 mL |
| Hoisin sauce | 1 tsp. | 5 mL |
| Cooking oil | 1 tsp. | 5 mL |
| Frozen Oriental mixed vegetables | 6 cups | 1.5 L |

Stir soy sauce into cornstarch in small bowl. Add next 7 ingredients. Stir well.

Heat large frying pan or wok on medium-high until very hot. Add cooking
oil. Add vegetables. Stir-fry for 2 minutes. Stir cornstarch mixture.
Add to vegetable mixture. Stir. Cook, covered, for 4 to 5 minutes
until vegetables are tender-crisp and sauce is boiling and thickened.
Makes about 3 cups (750 mL).

*1 cup (250 mL): 232 Calories; 4.7 g Total Fat (0.9 g Mono, 0.5 g Poly, 0.7 g Sat); 1 mg Cholesterol;*
*38 g Carbohydrate; 2 g Fibre; 8 g Protein; 1682 mg Sodium*

Pictured on page 71.

1. Orange Teriyaki Stir-Fry, above
2. Lemon Cranberry Couscous, page 69
3. Braised Red Cabbage, page 67

Props courtesy of: The Bay
Winners Stores

# Cucumber Chutney

*Fruit + curry + cucumber = delicious! The flavours are even more intense the second day. Best served with grilled pork or chicken.*

| | | |
|---|---|---|
| Cooking oil | 1/2 tsp. | 2 mL |
| Chopped onion | 1 cup | 250 mL |
| Chopped red pepper | 1 cup | 250 mL |
| Chopped dried apricot | 1/4 cup | 60 mL |
| Apple juice | 1/2 cup | 125 mL |
| Dried cranberries | 1/2 cup | 125 mL |
| Curry powder | 1 tsp. | 5 mL |
| Garlic powder | 1/4 tsp. | 1 mL |
| Ground cumin | 1/4 tsp. | 1 mL |
| Salt | 1/4 tsp. | 1 mL |
| Pepper | 1/8 tsp. | 0.5 mL |
| Diced peeled English cucumber | 1 1/3 cups | 325 mL |

Heat cooking oil in small saucepan on medium. Add onion and red pepper. Cook for about 5 minutes, stirring often, until onion starts to soften.

Add next 8 ingredients. Stir. Simmer, uncovered, for about 5 minutes until liquid is evaporated. Transfer to small bowl.

Add cucumber. Stir. Makes about 3 cups (750 mL).

*1/4 cup (60 mL): 40 Calories; 0.3 g Total Fat (0.1 g Mono, 0.1 g Poly ,trace Sat); 0 mg Cholesterol; 10 g Carbohydrate; 1 g Fibre; trace Protein; 52 mg Sodium*

Pictured on page 72.

1. Feta Polenta Muffins, page 74
2. Chili Biscuit Flower, page 75
3. Cucumber Chutney, above

Props courtesy of: Pier 1 Imports

# Feta Polenta Muffins

*Although this recipe doesn't use polenta, per se, the cornmeal and creamed corn combine for a perfect polenta flavour in this compact muffin. Serve with Chic Chicken Chili, page 106, or Chicken Mole, page 101.*

| | | |
|---|---|---|
| All-purpose flour | 1 cup | 250 mL |
| Yellow cornmeal | 1 cup | 250 mL |
| Baking soda | 1 tsp. | 5 mL |
| Dried basil | 1 tsp. | 5 mL |
| Salt | 1/4 tsp. | 1 mL |
| Pepper | 1/2 tsp. | 2 mL |
| Large eggs, fork-beaten | 2 | 2 |
| Can of cream-style corn | 10 oz. | 284 mL |
| Buttermilk (or soured milk, see Coach, page 42) | 1/2 cup | 125 mL |
| Cooking oil | 2 tbsp. | 30 mL |
| Hot pepper sauce | 1/4 tsp. | 1 mL |
| Can of sliced black olives, drained and chopped | 4 1/2 oz. | 125 mL |
| Crumbled feta cheese | 1/2 cup | 125 mL |

Preheat oven to 400°F (205°C). Measure first 6 ingredients into large bowl. Stir. Make a well in centre.

Combine next 5 ingredients in medium bowl. Add to well.

Add olives and feta. Stir until just moistened. Divide batter into 24 greased mini-muffin cups. Bake for about 15 minutes until wooden pick inserted in centre of muffin comes out clean. Let stand in pan for 5 minutes. Remove muffins from pan and place on wire rack to cool. Makes 24 mini-muffins.

*1 mini-muffin: 77 Calories; 2.8 g Total Fat (1.3 g Mono, 0.5 g Poly, 0.8 g Sat); 19 mg Cholesterol; 11 g Carbohydrate; 1 g Fibre; 2 g Protein; 187 mg Sodium*

Pictured on page 72.

Go-Withs

# Chili Biscuit Flower

*Giving flowers is always a great way to brighten someone's day.*
*This flower, although not your typical flora, is sure to put a smile on anyone's*
*face. Think of it as flower power. Serve with soups, chilies and salads.*

| | | |
|---|---|---|
| Tube of refrigerator country-style biscuits (10 biscuits per tube) | 12 oz. | 340 g |
| Butter (or hard margarine), melted | 1 tbsp. | 15 mL |
| Chili powder | 1/4 tsp. | 1 mL |
| Ground cumin | 1/8 tsp. | 0.5 mL |
| Grated Mexican cheese blend | 1/2 cup | 125 mL |
| Finely chopped fresh jalapeño pepper (see Coach, below) | 2 tbsp. | 30 mL |

Preheat oven to 400°F (205°C). Separate dough into 10 biscuits.
Place 1 biscuit in centre of greased 12 inch (30 cm) pizza pan.
Arrange remaining biscuits in circle around centre biscuit, with edges
touching. Gently press edges together and press biscuits out to 10 inch
(25 cm) circle.

Combine next 3 ingredients in small cup. Brush over biscuits.

Sprinkle with cheese and jalapeño pepper. Bake for about 12 minutes
until golden. Makes 10 biscuits.

*1 biscuit: 122 Calories; 4.9 g Total Fat (1.3 g Mono, 0.4 g Poly, 2.4 g Sat); 8 mg Cholesterol;
16 g Carbohydrate; trace Fibre; 3 g Protein; 277 mg Sodium*

Pictured on page 72.

COACH

Hot peppers contain capsaicin in the seeds and ribs.
Removing the seeds and ribs will reduce the heat.
Wear rubber gloves when handling hot peppers and avoid
touching your eyes. Wash your hands well afterwards.

# Italian Garlic Bread

*Just a few ordinary ingredients combine to make*
*top-notch garlic bread. Serve with pasta.*

| | | |
|---|---|---|
| Butter (or hard margarine), softened | 6 tbsp. | 100 mL |
| Grated Parmesan cheese | 1/4 cup | 60 mL |
| Garlic cloves, minced | 2 | 2 |
| (or 1/2 tsp., 2 mL, powder) | | |
| Italian seasoning | 2 tsp. | 10 mL |
| Italian (or French) bread loaf, | 1 | 1 |
| halved horizontally | | |

Preheat oven to 400°F (205°C). Combine first 4 ingredients in small bowl.

Spread butter mixture on cut sides of bread. Place, cut-side up, on ungreased baking sheet. Bake for about 15 minutes until heated through and toasted. Each half cuts into 16 pieces, for a total of 32 pieces.

*1 piece: 40 Calories; 3.3 g Total Fat (0.9 g Mono, 0.1 g Poly, 2.1 g Sat); 9 mg Cholesterol;*
*1 g Carbohydrate; trace Fibre; 2 g Protein; 93 mg Sodium*

Pictured on page 54.

# No-Salt Barbecue Spice

*This versatile seasoning mix can be used on chicken, pork or beef.*
*Store in an airtight container for up to three months.*

| | | |
|---|---|---|
| Brown sugar, packed | 1 tbsp. | 15 mL |
| Chili powder | 2 tsp. | 10 mL |
| Garlic powder | 2 tsp. | 10 mL |
| Paprika | 2 tsp. | 10 mL |
| Parsley flakes | 2 tsp. | 10 mL |
| Dried basil | 1 tsp. | 5 mL |
| Dried marjoram | 1 tsp. | 5 mL |
| Pepper | 1 tsp. | 5 mL |

Combine all 8 ingredients in small bowl. Makes about 1/3 cup (75 mL).

*1 tsp. (5 mL): 7 Calories; 0.1 g Total Fat (trace Mono, 0.1 g Poly, trace Sat); 0 mg Cholesterol;*
*2 g Carbohydrate; trace Fibre; trace Protein; 4 mg Sodium*

Go-Withs

# Tortilla Pesto Flutes

*These flavourful tortillas will be music to your mouth. Serve with soup or salad.*

| | | |
|---|---|---|
| Sun-dried tomato pesto | 16 tsp. | 80 mL |
| Flour tortillas (6 inch, 15 cm, diameter) | 8 | 8 |
| Chopped fresh basil | 3 tbsp. | 50 mL |

Cooking spray

Preheat oven to 350°F (175°C). Spread 2 tsp. (10 mL) pesto evenly over each tortilla, almost to edge. Sprinkle basil over top. Roll up tortillas, jelly-roll style. Place, seam-side down, on greased baking sheet with sides.

Spray tortillas with cooking spray. Bake for about 10 minutes until lightly browned and crisp. Makes 8 flutes.

*1 flute: 100 Calories; 2.1 g Total Fat (1.1 g Mono, 0.3 g Poly, 0.5 g Sat); 0 mg Cholesterol; 17 g Carbohydrate; 1 g Fibre; 3 g Protein; 244 mg Sodium*

# Spiced Sweet Pecans

*These nut-torious nibblies won't stay in your candy bowl for long! You can also use them for a salad topping.*

| | | |
|---|---|---|
| Granulated sugar | 3 tbsp. | 50 mL |
| Butter (or hard margarine), melted | 2 tbsp. | 30 mL |
| Balsamic vinegar | 1 tbsp. | 15 mL |
| Ground cinnamon | 1/2 tsp. | 2 mL |
| Paprika | 1/2 tsp. | 2 mL |
| Cayenne pepper | 1/4 tsp. | 1 mL |
| Salt | 1/4 tsp. | 1 mL |
| Pepper | 1/4 tsp. | 1 mL |
| Pecan halves | 2 1/2 cups | 625 mL |

Preheat oven to 350°F (175°C). Combine first 8 ingredients in large bowl.

Add pecans. Stir until coated. Transfer to baking sheet with sides, lined with greased foil. Bake for about 12 minutes until toasted and fragrant. Remove baking sheet to wire rack to cool. Makes about 2 1/2 cups (625 mL).

*1/4 cup (60 mL): 239 Calories; 23.4 g Total Fat (12.6 g Mono, 6.4 g Poly, 3.3 g Sat); 6 mg Cholesterol; 8 g Carbohydrate; 3 g Fibre; 3 g Protein; 75 mg Sodium*

Go-Withs

# Garlic Croutons

*These are so delicious and so quick and easy to make, those rock-hard boxed croutons will pale by comparison. Great in salads, soups or casseroles.*

| | | |
|---|---|---|
| Sourdough (or French) bread loaf | 1/2 | 1/2 |
| Butter (or hard margarine) | 2 tbsp. | 30 mL |
| Olive (or cooking) oil | 2 tbsp. | 30 mL |
| Garlic cloves, minced | 3 | 3 |
|   (or 3/4 tsp., 4 mL, powder) | | |
| Parsley flakes | 1/2 tsp. | 2 mL |
| Salt, sprinkle | | |
| Pepper, sprinkle | | |

Preheat oven to 325°F (160°C). Remove crust from bread. Cut bread into 1/2 inch (12 mm) slices. Stacking 2 or 3 slices together, cut into 1/2 inch (12 mm) cubes. Transfer bread cubes to extra-large bowl.

Heat and stir next 4 ingredients in large frying pan on medium until butter is melted. Drizzle half of butter mixture over bread cubes. Toss. Drizzle with remaining butter mixture. Toss until coated. Spread evenly on ungreased baking sheet with sides.

Sprinkle with salt and pepper. Bake for about 20 minutes until crisp and golden. Remove baking sheet to wire rack to cool. Makes about 4 cups (1 L).

*1/4 cup (60 mL): 31 Calories; 3.1 g Total Fat (1.6 g Mono, 0.2 g Poly, 1.1 g Sat); 4 mg Cholesterol; 1 g Carbohydrate; trace Fibre; trace Protein; 18 mg Sodium*

**Variation:** Sprinkle with various dried herbs for herb-seasoned croutons.

# Speedy Sassy Salsa

*This fresh pepper-packed salsa is sassy, indeed! The heat lingers and won't disappoint. If you can, make this salsa a day in advance to let the flavours really develop—but it's still delicious when it's brand spankin' fresh. Serve with tortilla chips or grilled meats. Store in an airtight container in the fridge for up to four days.*

| | | |
|---|---|---|
| Small green peppers, coarsely chopped | 2 | 2 |
| Small onion, cut into 4 pieces | 1 | 1 |
| Coarsely chopped fresh cilantro or parsley, lightly packed | 1/2 cup | 125 mL |
| Fresh jalapeño peppers (see Coach, page 75), coarsely chopped | 2 | 2 |
| Garlic clove | 1 | 1 |
| Can of diced tomatoes (with juice) | 28 oz. | 796 mL |
| Can of tomato paste | 5 1/2 oz. | 156 mL |
| Lime juice | 3 tbsp. | 50 mL |
| Ground cumin | 1 tsp. | 5 mL |
| Hot sauce (optional) | 1 tsp. | 5 mL |

Put first 5 ingredients into blender or food processor. Process with on/off motion until finely chopped. Transfer to large bowl.

Put remaining 5 ingredients into blender or food processor. Process until smooth. Add to vegetable mixture. Stir. Makes about 6 cups (1.5 L).

*1/4 cup (60 mL): 18 Calories; 0.1 g Total Fat (trace Mono, trace Poly, trace Sat); 0 mg Cholesterol; 4 g Carbohydrate; 1 g Fibre; 1 g Protein; 102 mg Sodium*

Pictured on page 17.

**COACH**

If a recipe calls for less than an entire can of tomato paste, freeze the unopened can for 30 minutes. Open both ends and push the contents through one end. Slice off only what you need. Freeze the remaining paste in a resealable freezer bag or plastic wrap for future use.

# Lemon Pepper Muffins

*The peppery bursts of flavour in these fresh-tasting lemon muffins make
them a perfect companion for fish or seafood soups and salads. If you don't
have seasoned salt, table salt can be used in a pinch.*

| | | |
|---|---|---|
| All-purpose flour | 2 1/4 cups | 550 mL |
| Baking powder | 2 1/2 tsp. | 12 mL |
| Pepper | 1 1/2 tsp. | 7 mL |
| Seasoned salt | 1/4 tsp. | 1 mL |
| Large eggs, fork-beaten | 3 | 3 |
| Milk | 2/3 cup | 150 mL |
| Butter (or hard margarine), melted | 1/2 cup | 125 mL |
| Granulated sugar | 1/4 cup | 60 mL |
| Lemon juice | 3 tbsp. | 50 mL |
| Grated lemon zest (see Coach, below) | 2 tsp. | 10 mL |
| Chopped green onion | 1/4 cup | 60 mL |

Preheat oven to 400°F (205°C). Measure first 4 ingredients into medium
bowl. Stir. Make a well in centre.

Combine next 6 ingredients in small bowl. Add to well.

Add green onion. Stir until just moistened. Fill 24 greased mini-muffin cups
3/4 full. Bake for about 12 minutes until wooden pick inserted in centre
of muffin comes out clean. Let stand in pan for 5 minutes. Remove muffins
from pan and place on wire rack to cool. Make 24 mini-muffins.

*1 mini-muffin: 93 Calories; 4.5 g Total Fat (1.3 g Mono, 0.2 g Poly, 2.6 g Sat); 34 mg Cholesterol;
11 g Carbohydrate; trace Fibre; 2 g Protein; 80 mg Sodium*

Pictured on page 89.

When a recipe calls for grated lemon zest and juice,
it's easier to grate the lemon first, then juice it. Be careful
not to grate down to the pith (white part of the peel),
which is bitter and best avoided.

Go-Withs

# Lemon Butter Sauce

*This little go-with is so unexpected that your guests will surely feel pampered.*
*Serve warm with muffins, pancakes, waffles, ice cream—even grilled chicken!*

| | | |
|---|---|---|
| Granulated sugar | 1/2 cup | 125 mL |
| Cornstarch | 2 tbsp. | 30 mL |
| Grated lemon zest | 1/2 tsp. | 2 mL |
| Water | 1 cup | 250 mL |
| Lemon juice | 2 tbsp. | 30 mL |
| Butter | 2 tbsp. | 30 mL |

Combine first 3 ingredients in small saucepan.

Add water and lemon juice. Heat and stir until boiling and thickened. Remove from heat.

Add butter. Stir until melted. Makes about 1 1/3 cups (325 mL).

*2 tbsp. (30 mL): 60 Calories; 2.1 g Total Fat (0.6 g Mono, 0.1 g Poly, 1.3 g Sat); 6 mg Cholesterol; 11 g Carbohydrate; trace Fibre; trace Protein; 15 mg Sodium*

# Creamy Horseradish Sauce

*Perk up burgers, roast beef or even mashed potatoes with this flavourful sauce.*
*Store in an airtight container in the fridge for up to a week.*

| | | |
|---|---|---|
| Block of cream cheese, softened | 8 oz. | 250 g |
| Prepared horseradish | 2 tbsp. | 30 mL |
| Lemon juice | 1 tbsp. | 15 mL |
| Granulated sugar | 1 tsp. | 5 mL |
| Salt | 1/4 tsp. | 1 mL |
| Milk | 1/3 cup | 75 mL |
| Chopped fresh chives | 1 tbsp. | 15 mL |

Beat first 5 ingredients in medium bowl, scraping down sides if necessary, until smooth.

Slowly add milk, beating constantly, until combined. Add chives. Stir. Makes about 2 cups (500 mL).

*2 tbsp. (30 mL): 52 Calories; 4.8 g Total Fat (1.4 g Mono, 0.2 g Poly, 3.0 g Sat); 15 mg Cholesterol; 1 g Carbohydrate; trace Fibre; 1 g Protein; 84 mg Sodium*

Go-Withs

# Blueberry Maple Topping

*Perfect with pancakes or ice cream. Will keep in the fridge for two weeks.*

| | | |
|---|---|---|
| Water | 2 tbsp. | 30 mL |
| Cornstarch | 2 tsp. | 10 mL |
| Fresh (or frozen) blueberries | 1 1/2 cups | 375 mL |
| Granulated sugar | 1/4 cup | 60 mL |
| Maple (or maple-flavoured) syrup | 1/4 cup | 60 mL |

Stir water into cornstarch in small cup.

Combine remaining 3 ingredients in small saucepan. Bring to a boil on medium. Reduce heat to medium-low. Simmer, uncovered, for about 5 minutes, stirring occasionally, until blueberries are soft. Stir cornstarch mixture. Add to blueberry mixture. Heat and stir until boiling and thickened. Makes about 1 1/4 cups (300 mL).

*1/4 cup (60 mL): 104 Calories; 0.3 g Total Fat (trace Mono, trace Poly, trace Sat); 0 mg Cholesterol; 26 g Carbohydrate; 1 g Fibre; trace Protein; 2 mg Sodium*

# Tomato Basil Sauce

*Make your own tomato sauce. Great with pasta, chicken or fish.*

| | | |
|---|---|---|
| Olive (or cooking) oil | 1 tbsp. | 15 mL |
| Chopped onion | 1 cup | 250 mL |
| Dried basil | 2 tsp. | 10 mL |
| Garlic cloves, minced | 2 | 2 |
| (or 1/2 tsp., 2 mL, powder) | | |
| Can of diced tomatoes (with juice) | 28 oz. | 796 mL |
| Balsamic vinegar | 1 tbsp. | 15 mL |
| Granulated sugar | 1 tsp. | 5 mL |
| Salt | 1/2 tsp. | 2 mL |
| Pepper | 1/4 tsp. | 1 mL |

Heat olive oil in medium saucepan on medium. Add next 3 ingredients. Cook, uncovered, for about 5 minutes, stirring often, until onion is softened.

Add remaining 5 ingredients. Stir. Bring to a boil on medium. Cook for 5 minutes, stirring occasionally, to blend flavours. Carefully process with hand blender or in blender until smooth. Makes about 3 1/2 cups (875 mL).

*1/2 cup (125 mL): 51 Calories; 2.0 g Total Fat (1.4 g Mono, 0.2 g Poly, 0.3 g Sat); 0 mg Cholesterol; 8 g Carbohydrate; trace Fibre; 1 g Protein; 478 mg Sodium*

Go-Withs

# Kickin' Shrimp Sauce

*This spicy, sweet and tangy cocktail sauce will knock your socks off.*
*Serve alongside chilled cooked shrimp or crispy fish fillets. Store in an airtight*
*container in the refrigerator for up to 10 days—if it lasts that long!*

| | | |
|---|---|---|
| Chili sauce | 1/2 cup | 125 mL |
| Creamed horseradish | 2 1/2 tbsp. | 37 mL |
| Lemon juice | 2 tbsp. | 30 mL |
| Grated lemon zest | 1/2 tsp. | 2 mL |

Combine all 4 ingredients in small bowl. Makes about 3/4 cup (175 mL).

*2 tbsp. (30 mL): 10 Calories; 0.1 g Total Fat (trace Mono, trace Poly, trace Sat); 0 mg Cholesterol;*
*2 g Carbohydrate; 1 g Fibre; trace Protein; 26 mg Sodium*

# Honey Basil Vinaigrette

*Make your everyday mixed greens special by adding this*
*sweet and savoury homemade dressing.*

| | | |
|---|---|---|
| Olive (or cooking) oil | 2/3 cup | 150 mL |
| Apple cider vinegar | 3 tbsp. | 50 mL |
| Apple juice | 3 tbsp. | 50 mL |
| Chopped fresh basil | 2 tbsp. | 30 mL |
|   (or 1 1/2 tsp., 7 mL, dried) | | |
| Liquid honey | 1 tbsp. | 15 mL |
| Dry mustard | 1 tsp. | 5 mL |
| Salt | 1/4 tsp. | 1 mL |

Combine all 7 ingredients in jar with tight-fitting lid. Shake well.
Makes about 1 cup (250 mL).

*2 tbsp. (30 mL): 159 Calories; 16.6 g Total Fat (12.2 g Mono, 1.4 g Poly, 2.2 g Sat);*
*0 mg Cholesterol; 3 g Carbohydrate; trace Fibre; trace Protein; 69 mg Sodium*

**COACH**

If you're a big fan of fresh herbs, try adding a little fresh
basil to your greens for an added layer of freshness.

# Basic Beef Sukiyaki

*Everyone needs a quick and easy stir-fry in their cooking repertoire.
Get some rice cooking right away so you have something to put your sukiyaki
on. And if you'd rather leave the spinach to the Popeyes of the world,
use half a head of Chinese cabbage, cut into short pieces, instead.*

| | | |
|---|---|---|
| Prepared beef broth | 1/3 cup | 75 mL |
| Brown sugar, packed | 1/4 cup | 60 mL |
| Soy sauce | 3 tbsp. | 50 mL |
| Cornstarch | 1 1/2 tsp. | 7 mL |
| Cooking oil | 2 tsp. | 10 mL |
| Beef top sirloin steak, cut into thin, short strips | 1 lb. | 454 g |
| Box of frozen chopped spinach, thawed and squeezed dry | 10 oz. | 300 g |
| Sliced fresh white mushrooms | 1 cup | 250 mL |
| Green onions, chopped | 4 | 4 |

Heat large frying pan or wok on medium-high until very hot.
Meanwhile, combine first 4 ingredients in small bowl. Set aside.

Add cooking oil to frying pan. Add beef. Stir-fry for 2 to 4 minutes until
desired doneness.

Add remaining 3 ingredients. Stir-fry for about 2 minutes until liquid
is evaporated. Stir cornstarch mixture. Add to beef mixture. Stir well.
Reduce heat to medium. Heat and stir for about 1 minute until boiling
and thickened. Makes about 4 cups (1 L).

*1 cup (250 mL): 296 Calories; 10.7 g Total Fat (4.6 g Mono, 1.0 g Poly, 3.3 g Sat);
60 mg Cholesterol; 22 g Carbohydrate; 2 g Fibre; 29 g Protein; 822 mg Sodium*

**TOFU SUKIYAKI:** Use same amount of cubed firm tofu instead of beef.

# Feel Good Cheeseburger Macaroni

*Had a hard day? This is the ultimate comfort food.*
*And if you want to spice things up a bit, use cans of seasoned*
*tomatoes—there are quite a few varieties out there.*

| | | |
|---|---|---|
| Water | 8 cups | 2 L |
| Salt | 1 tsp. | 5 mL |
| Elbow macaroni | 2 cups | 500 mL |
| Cooking oil | 1 tsp. | 5 mL |
| Lean ground beef | 1 lb. | 454 g |
| Chopped onion | 1 cup | 250 mL |
| Garlic clove, minced | 1 | 1 |
| (or 1/4 tsp., 1 mL, powder) | | |
| Cans of stewed tomatoes | 2 | 2 |
| (14 oz., 398 mL, each), coarsely chopped | | |
| Ketchup | 1/4 cup | 60 mL |
| Italian seasoning | 1/2 tsp. | 2 mL |
| Salt | 1/2 tsp. | 2 mL |
| Pepper | 1/2 tsp. | 2 mL |
| Grated sharp Cheddar cheese | 1 cup | 250 mL |
| Grated sharp Cheddar cheese | 1/2 cup | 125 mL |

Combine water and salt in large saucepan. Bring to a boil. Add macaroni.
Boil, uncovered, for 6 to 8 minutes, stirring occasionally, until tender
but firm. Drain. Cover to keep warm.

Meanwhile, heat cooking oil in large frying pan on medium-high.
Add next 3 ingredients. Scramble-fry for 8 to 10 minutes until beef
is browned. Drain.

Add next 5 ingredients. Stir. Bring to a boil. Reduce heat to medium.
Cook for 5 minutes to blend flavours.

Add first amount of cheese and macaroni. Cook and stir for about
2 minutes until heated through. Remove from heat.

Sprinkle with second amount of cheese. Makes about 8 1/2 cups (2.1 L).

*1 cup (250 mL): 335 Calories; 13.0 g Total Fat (4.6 g Mono, 0.7 g Poly, 6.6 g Sat);*
*63 mg Cholesterol; 28 g Carbohydrate; 1 g Fibre; 26 g Protein; 623 mg Sodium*

**Variation:** Use Mexican or Italian cheese blend instead of Cheddar.

# Pineapple Meatballs

*Meatballs can be very chic when they're flavoured with ginger
and soy sauce, and are served over a bed of rice. Just get your rice cooking
while you make the meatballs.*

| | | |
|---|---|---|
| Large egg, fork-beaten | 1 | 1 |
| Fine dry bread crumbs | 3/4 cup | 175 mL |
| Milk | 1/4 cup | 60 mL |
| Soy sauce | 1 tbsp. | 15 mL |
| Finely grated gingerroot | 2 tsp. | 10 mL |
| (or 1/2 tsp., 2 mL, ground ginger) | | |
| Garlic cloves, minced | 2 | 2 |
| (or 1/2 tsp., 2 mL, powder) | | |
| Lean ground beef | 1 lb. | 454 g |
| Cooking oil | 1 tsp. | 5 mL |
| Chopped green pepper | 1/2 cup | 125 mL |
| Can of pineapple tidbits (with juice) | 14 oz. | 398 mL |
| Brown sugar, packed | 1/3 cup | 75 mL |
| Rice vinegar | 1/4 cup | 60 mL |
| Hoisin sauce | 2 tbsp. | 30 mL |
| Water | 2 tbsp. | 30 mL |
| Cornstarch | 1 tbsp. | 15 mL |

Preheat oven to 400°F (205°C). Combine first 6 ingredients in large bowl.

Add beef. Mix well. Roll into 1 1/2 inch (3.8 cm) balls. Arrange on greased baking sheet with sides. Bake for 15 minutes. Makes about 24 meatballs.

Meanwhile, heat cooking oil in large frying pan on medium-high. Add green pepper. Cook for 2 to 4 minutes, stirring occasionally, until tender-crisp.

Combine next 4 ingredients in small bowl. Add to green pepper. Add meatballs. Stir. Reduce heat to medium-low. Simmer, covered, for about 3 minutes until meatballs are fully cooked and internal temperature reaches 160°F (71°C).

Stir water into cornstarch in small cup. Add to meatball mixture. Heat and stir for about 2 minutes until boiling and thickened. Makes about 5 cups (1.25 L).

*(continued on next page)*

*1 cup (250 mL): 402 Calories; 15.6 g Total Fat (7.0 g Mono, 1.0 g Poly, 5.7 g Sat); 92 mg Cholesterol; 42 g Carbohydrate; 2 g Fibre; 22 g Protein; 490 mg Sodium*

Meat thermometers are great investments for any cook, but especially rookie cooks. With their clearly labelled temperatures, they let you know, for sure, that your meat is properly cooked.

# Your Best Barbecued Steak

*Nothing wins rave reviews from both the ladies
and the men like a fantastic barbecued steak.*

| | | |
|---|---|---|
| **Cooking oil** | **2 tsp.** | **10 mL** |
| **Dijon mustard** | **2 tsp.** | **10 mL** |
| **No-Salt Barbecue Spice, page 76** | **1 1/2 tsp.** | **7 mL** |
| **Beef rib-eye steak** | **1 lb.** | **454 g** |

Preheat gas barbecue to medium-high. Combine first 3 ingredients in small cup.

Rub both sides of steak with mustard mixture. Cook on greased grill for 4 to 5 minutes per side until desired doneness. Transfer to plate. Cover with foil. Let stand for 5 minutes. Cut into 4 equal portions. Serves 4.

*1 serving: 241 Calories; 15.9 g Total Fat (6.9 g Mono, 1.2 g Poly, 5.5 g Sat); 102 mg Cholesterol; 1 g Carbohydrate; trace Fibre; 22 g Protein; 79 mg Sodium*

Pictured on page 90.

To assess doneness of a steak, follow these guidelines:
**rare:** seared with a 75 per cent red inside
**medium rare:** seared with a 50 per cent red inside
**medium:** seared with a 25 per cent pink inside
**medium well:** cooked throughout with a hint of pink
        in the middle
**well done:** no hint of pink on the inside

# Mega Meatball Sandwiches

*You can spice up this cheesy bad boy by adding 1/4 to 1/2 tsp.*
*(1 to 2 mL) dried crushed chilies to the sauce.*

| | | |
|---|---|---|
| Cooking oil | 1 tsp. | 5 mL |
| Chopped onion | 1/2 cup | 125 mL |
| Can of tomato sauce | 14 oz. | 398 mL |
| Bay leaves | 2 | 2 |
| Italian seasoning | 1 1/2 tsp. | 7 mL |
| Pepper | 1/4 tsp. | 1 mL |
| Frozen cooked meatballs | 32 | 32 |
| Baguette bread loaf | 1 | 1 |
| Grated Mexican cheese blend | 1 cup | 250 mL |

Heat cooking oil in large frying pan on medium. Add onion. Cook for about 5 minutes, stirring often, until onion starts to soften.

Add next 4 ingredients. Stir.

Add meatballs. Stir. Simmer, covered, for about 8 minutes, stirring occasionally, until heated through. Discard bay leaves.

Preheat broiler. Cut baguette crosswise into 4 equal portions. Cut portions horizontally lengthwise almost, but not quite through, to other side. Place, cut-side up, on ungreased baking sheet with sides. Spoon meatball mixture over top. Sprinkle with cheese. Broil on top rack in oven for 2 to 4 minutes until cheese is melted. Makes 4 sandwiches.

*1 sandwich: 674 Calories; 39.2 g Total Fat (13.3 g Mono, 1.8 g Poly, 16.4 g Sat); 211 mg Cholesterol; 32 g Carbohydrate; 3 g Fibre; 46 g Protein; 1183 mg Sodium*

Pictured on page 17.

1. Lemon Pepper Muffins, page 80
2. Thoroughly Modern Chili, page 116
3. Berry Cake Cups, page 136

Props courtesy of:  Pier 1 Imports
                    Winners Stores

# Tater Surprise

*When we say trouble-free, we mean trouble-free—*
*you can even serve this one straight out of the frying pan!*

| | | |
|---|---|---|
| Frozen potato tots (gems or puffs) | 40 | 40 |
| Cooking oil | 1 tsp. | 5 mL |
| Lean ground beef | 1 lb. | 454 g |
| Chopped onion | 1/4 cup | 60 mL |
| Frozen mixed peas and carrots | 2 cups | 500 mL |
| Can of condensed cream of mushroom soup | 10 oz. | 284 mL |
| Barbecue sauce | 2 tbsp. | 30 mL |

Preheat oven to 450°F (230°C). Arrange potato tots in single layer on ungreased baking sheet with sides. Bake for about 15 minutes until golden.

Meanwhile, heat cooking oil in large frying pan on medium-high. Add beef and onion. Scramble-fry for 8 to 10 minutes until beef is browned. Drain.

Add remaining 3 ingredients. Stir. Arrange potato tots in single layer over beef mixture. Reduce heat to medium. Cook for 2 to 3 minutes until bubbling and vegetables are tender. Serves 4.

*1 serving: 536 Calories; 24.0 g Total Fat (8.5 g Mono, 0.9 g Poly, 6.9 g Sat); 92 mg Cholesterol; 39 g Carbohydrate; 6 g Fibre; 40 g Protein; 1162 mg Sodium*

1. Thai-rrific Basil Stir-Fry, page 93
2. Your Best Barbecued Steak, page 87
3. Cheesy Portobellos, page 92

Props courtesy of: Pier 1 Imports
Winners Stores

# Cheesy Portobellos

*Now this is the kind of entree you'd expect to see in a very popular, big-city bistro. With its smoky bacon flavour, feta and Brie cheese, no one's going to believe it was made by a rookie.*

| | | |
|---|---|---|
| Portobello mushrooms (about 4 inch, 10 cm, diameter), stems removed | 4 | 4 |
| Salt | 1/4 tsp. | 1 mL |
| Pepper | 1/4 tsp. | 1 mL |
| Lean ground beef | 1/2 lb. | 225 g |
| Chopped onion | 1/2 cup | 125 mL |
| Bacon slices, chopped | 4 | 4 |
| Garlic clove, minced (or 1/4 tsp., 1 mL, powder) | 1 | 1 |
| Brie cheese round, chopped | 4 oz. | 125 g |
| Crumbled feta cheese | 1/2 cup | 125 mL |
| Chopped fresh basil | 2 tbsp. | 30 mL |
| Finely chopped chipotle pepper in adobo sauce (see Coach, page 133) | 1/2 tsp. | 2 mL |

Preheat oven to 400°F (205°C). Using small spoon, remove and discard gills from mushroom caps. Sprinkle with salt and pepper. Place in greased 9 x 13 inch (22 x 33 cm) pan. Bake for about 8 minutes until starting to soften.

Meanwhile, heat large frying pan on medium-high. Add next 4 ingredients. Scramble-fry for 8 to 10 minutes until bacon is almost crisp and beef is browned. Drain.

Add remaining 4 ingredients. Stir. Preheat broiler. Spoon beef mixture into mushrooms. Broil on centre rack in oven for about 5 minutes until filling is bubbling and golden. Makes 4 stuffed mushrooms.

*1 stuffed mushroom: 349 Calories; 21.2 g Total Fat (7.1 g Mono, 0.9 g Poly, 11.6 g Sat); 99 mg Cholesterol; 8 g Carbohydrate; 2 g Fibre; 31 g Protein; 742 mg Sodium*

Pictured on page 90.

# Thai-rrific Basil Stir-Fry

*Have someone you want to impress? Here's a hint: because*
*Thai flavours taste exotic, people automatically think Thai dishes*
*are hard to make. Serve this one over rice.*

| | | |
|---|---|---|
| Prepared beef broth | 1/4 cup | 60 mL |
| Lime juice | 2 tbsp. | 30 mL |
| Brown sugar, packed | 2 tbsp. | 30 mL |
| Soy sauce | 1 tbsp. | 15 mL |
| Cornstarch | 2 tsp. | 10 mL |
| Cooking oil | 1 tbsp. | 15 mL |
| Beef top sirloin steak, cut into thin, short strips | 1 lb. | 454 g |
| Garlic clove, minced (or 1/4 tsp., 1 mL, powder) | 1 | 1 |
| Dried crushed chilies | 1 tsp. | 5 mL |
| Sliced onion | 1 cup | 250 mL |
| Sliced red pepper | 1 cup | 250 mL |
| Chopped fresh basil | 1/4 cup | 60 mL |
| Chopped dry-roasted peanuts (optional) | 1/4 cup | 60 mL |

Heat large frying pan or wok on medium-high until very hot.
Meanwhile, combine first 5 ingredients in small cup. Set aside.

Add cooking oil to frying pan. Add next 3 ingredients. Stir-fry for about
2 to 4 minutes until beef reaches desired doneness. Transfer to plate.
Cover to keep warm.

Add onion and red pepper to same frying pan. Stir-fry for about 2 minutes
until tender-crisp. Add beef mixture. Stir cornstarch mixture. Add to beef
mixture. Heat and stir for about 1 minute until boiling and thickened.

Add basil. Stir. Sprinkle peanuts over top. Makes about 2 1/2 cups
(625 mL). Serves 4.

*1 serving: 217 Calories; 7.1 g Total Fat (3.1 g Mono, trace Poly, 2.8 g Sat); 60 mg Cholesterol;*
*14 g Carbohydrate; 1 g Fibre; 23 g Protein; 325 mg Sodium*

Pictured on page 90.

# Lazy Lasagna

*This lasagna isn't lacking motivation—you're the one who gets to be lazy! It isn't baked or layered—but the taste is all lasagna! Double the amount of chilies if you like a little heat.*

| | | |
|---|---|---|
| Water | 8 cups | 2 L |
| Salt | 1 tsp. | 5 mL |
| Lasagna noodles, broken into 4 pieces each | 8 | 8 |
| Cooking oil | 1 tbsp. | 15 mL |
| Sliced fresh white mushrooms | 2 cups | 500 mL |
| Chopped green pepper | 1 cup | 250 mL |
| Chopped onion | 1 cup | 250 mL |
| Dried crushed chilies | 1/2 tsp. | 2 mL |
| Tomato pasta sauce | 2 cups | 500 mL |
| Can of diced tomatoes (with juice) | 14 oz. | 398 mL |
| Frozen cooked meatballs | 20 | 20 |
| Dried oregano | 1 tsp. | 5 mL |
| Dried basil | 1/2 tsp. | 2 mL |
| Pepper | 1/4 tsp. | 1 mL |
| Grated mozzarella cheese | 2 cups | 500 mL |

Combine water and salt in large saucepan or Dutch oven. Bring to a boil. Add noodles. Boil, uncovered, for about 10 minutes, stirring occasionally, until tender but firm. Drain. Return to same pot. Cover to keep warm.

Meanwhile, heat cooking oil in large frying pan on medium-high. Add next 4 ingredients. Cook for about 5 minutes, stirring occasionally, until onion is softened.

Add next 6 ingredients. Stir. Bring to a boil. Reduce heat to medium. Cook, covered, for about 5 minutes until heated through. Add noodles. Stir.

Preheat broiler. Sprinkle cheese over noodle mixture. Broil on centre rack in oven (see Coach, page 95) for about 5 minutes until cheese is melted and golden. Serves 4.

*1 serving: 810 Calories; 35.4 g Total Fat (13.8 g Mono, 2.5 g Poly, 14.7 g Sat); 162 mg Cholesterol; 75 g Carbohydrate; 6 g Fibre; 48 g Protein; 1378 mg Sodium*

# Stroganoff Noodles

*Named after Russian nobility, beef Stroganoff is a rich and decadent delight.
Add some steamed veggies and dinner is served. (Save the leftover onion soup
mix for other recipes. Or you can rub it on a roast before cooking
for a quick and easy seasoning.)*

| | | |
|---|---|---|
| Water | 12 cups | 3 L |
| Salt | 1 1/2 tsp. | 7 mL |
| Medium egg noodles | 7 cups | 1.75 L |
| Cooking oil | 1 tsp. | 5 mL |
| Lean ground beef | 1 lb. | 454 g |
| Can of condensed cream of mushroom soup | 10 oz. | 284 mL |
| Milk | 1 cup | 250 mL |
| Dry onion soup mix (stir before measuring) | 2 tbsp. | 30 mL |
| Sour cream | 1/2 cup | 125 mL |

**Chopped fresh dill, for garnish**

Combine water and salt in Dutch oven. Bring to a boil. Add noodles.
Boil, uncovered, for 5 to 6 minutes, stirring occasionally, until tender
but firm. Drain. Return to same pot. Cover to keep warm.

Meanwhile, heat cooking oil in large frying pan on medium-high.
Add beef. Scramble-fry for 8 to 10 minutes until browned. Drain.
Reduce heat to medium.

Stir next 3 ingredients in small bowl until smooth. Add to beef.
Cook for about 5 minutes, stirring occasionally, until boiling
and thickened.

Add sour cream and noodles. Stir well.

Garnish with dill. Makes about 10 cups (2.5 L).

*1 cup (250 mL): 775 Calories; 15.5 g Total Fat (3.2 g Mono, 2.4 g Poly, 5.6 g Sat);
208 mg Cholesterol; 119 g Carbohydrate; 5 g Fibre; 39 g Protein; 562 mg Sodium*

**COACH** When baking or broiling food in a frying pan with a handle
that isn't ovenproof, wrap the handle in tinfoil and keep
it to the front of the oven, away from the element.

# Crispy Chicken Cutlets

*These crisp, juicy golden brown cutlets are packed with flavour. Don't be afraid to try this versatile coating on pork or turkey cutlets, as well.*

| | | |
|---|---|---|
| All-purpose flour | 1/3 cup | 75 mL |
| Large eggs, fork-beaten | 2 | 2 |
| Milk | 2 tbsp. | 30 mL |
| Fine dry bread crumbs | 3/4 cup | 175 mL |
| Paprika | 2 tsp. | 10 mL |
| Salt | 1 tsp. | 5 mL |
| Pepper | 1 tsp. | 5 mL |
| Garlic powder | 1/2 tsp. | 2 mL |
| Ground cinnamon | 1/4 tsp. | 1 mL |
| Cooking oil | 2 tbsp. | 30 mL |
| Chicken breast cutlets (about 1 lb., 454 g) | 4 | 4 |
| Chopped fresh parsley | 2 tbsp. | 30 mL |

Measure flour onto large plate.

Beat eggs and milk with fork in large shallow dish.

Combine next 6 ingredients in small cup. Transfer to separate large plate.

Heat cooking oil in large frying pan on medium. Press both sides of chicken into flour. Dip into egg mixture. Press both sides of chicken into crumb mixture until coated. Discard any remaining flour, egg mixture and bread crumb mixture. Arrange chicken in frying pan. Cook for about 5 minutes per side until golden and no longer pink inside.

Sprinkle with parsley. Makes 4 cutlets.

*1 cutlet: 392 Calories; 15.0 g Total Fat (7.2 g Mono, 3.8 g Poly, 2.8 g Sat); 173 mg Cholesterol; 19 g Carbohydrate; 1 g Fibre; 43 g Protein; 686 mg Sodium*

# South Seas Chicken

*Ahoy, matey! There'll be no mutiny when your guests taste this sweet-and-spicy bounty. Serve on rice, couscous or chickpeas.*

| | | |
|---|---|---|
| Pineapple juice | 1 cup | 250 mL |
| Apple cider vinegar | 2 tbsp. | 30 mL |
| Lime juice | 2 tbsp. | 30 mL |
| Brown sugar, packed | 1 tbsp. | 15 mL |
| Cornstarch | 2 tsp. | 10 mL |
| Garlic powder | 1 tsp. | 5 mL |
| Ground cinnamon | 1 tsp. | 5 mL |
| Ground ginger | 1 tsp. | 5 mL |
| Ground allspice | 1/2 tsp. | 2 mL |
| Cayenne pepper | 1/8 tsp. | 0.5 mL |
| Cooking oil | 2 tsp. | 10 mL |
| Boneless, skinless chicken thighs, cut into bite-sized pieces | 1 lb. | 454 g |

Chopped fresh parsley, for garnish

Combine first 10 ingredients in small bowl.

Heat large frying pan on medium-high until very hot. Add cooking oil. Add chicken. Stir-fry for about 5 minutes until chicken is no longer pink inside. Reduce heat to medium-low. Add pineapple juice mixture. Heat and stir until boiling and thickened.

Garnish with parsley. Makes about 2 1/2 cups (625 mL).

*1 cup (250 mL): 390 Calories; 16.1 g Total Fat (6.7 g Mono, 4.0 g Poly, 3.6 g Sat); 122 mg Cholesterol; 26 g Carbohydrate; 1 g Fibre; 34 g Protein; 120 mg Sodium*

COACH

Wondering if you have to be specific with the cut of chicken when you're making dishes like these? No! You can easily substitute other cuts, as long as you keep the boneless weight the same.

# Easy Quesadillas

*Want to add an extra dimension to these fresh and flavourful quesadillas (pronounced keh-sah-DEE-yahs)? Try using any of the different flavoured tortillas available at your supermarket. Serve with salsa and sour cream, and add a big green salad for a complete meal.*

| | | |
|---|---|---|
| Cooking oil | 1 tsp. | 5 mL |
| Sliced fresh white mushrooms | 2 cups | 500 mL |
| Chopped green pepper | 2/3 cup | 150 mL |
| Chopped onion | 1/3 cup | 75 mL |
| Chopped cooked chicken (see Coach, page 31) | 1 1/2 cups | 375 mL |
| Basil pesto | 1/4 cup | 60 mL |
| Flour tortillas (9 inch, 22 cm, diameter) | 4 | 4 |
| Grated mozzarella cheese | 1 1/3 cups | 325 mL |
| Crumbled feta cheese | 3/4 cup | 175 mL |
| Cooking spray | | |

Preheat oven to 425°F (220°C). Heat cooking oil in large frying pan on medium. Add next 3 ingredients. Cook for 8 to 10 minutes, stirring often, until onion is softened and liquid is evaporated.

Add chicken and pesto. Stir.

Spoon chicken mixture evenly over half of each tortilla.

Sprinkle mozzarella and feta cheese over chicken mixture. Fold tortillas in half to cover filling. Press down lightly. Arrange tortillas on greased baking sheet with sides.

Spray tortillas with cooking spray. Bake for about 10 minutes until crisp and starting to brown. Cut tortillas in half. Makes 8 wedges.

*1 wedge: 296 Calories; 17.5 g Total Fat (5.1 g Mono, 2.8 g Poly, 7.0 g Sat); 68 mg Cholesterol; 13 g Carbohydrate; 1 g Fibre; 21 g Protein; 478 mg Sodium*

# First-Class Chicken Curry

*Mango and peaches add a gentle sweetness to this delicious chicken curry served over a bed of rice. Start the rice cooking before you start preparing the curry.*

| | | |
|---|---|---|
| Water | 3 cups | 750 mL |
| Salt | 1/2 tsp. | 2 mL |
| Long grain white rice | 1 1/2 cups | 375 mL |
| Cooking oil | 1 tbsp. | 15 mL |
| Lean ground chicken | 1 lb. | 454 g |
| Chopped onion | 1/2 cup | 125 mL |
| Coleslaw mix | 2 cups | 500 mL |
| Mango chutney, larger pieces chopped | 1/2 cup | 125 mL |
| Prepared chicken broth | 1/2 cup | 125 mL |
| Curry powder | 1 tsp. | 5 mL |
| Finely grated gingerroot | 1 tsp. | 5 mL |
| (or 1/4 tsp., 1 mL, ground ginger) | | |
| Garlic powder | 1/4 tsp. | 1 mL |
| Ground cumin | 1/4 tsp. | 1 mL |
| Can of sliced peaches in juice, | 14 oz. | 398 mL |
| drained and chopped | | |
| Plain yogurt | 1/2 cup | 125 mL |

Combine water and salt in medium saucepan. Bring to a boil. Add rice. Stir. Reduce heat to medium-low. Simmer, covered, for about 20 minutes, without stirring, until liquid is absorbed. Remove from heat. Let stand, covered, for 5 minutes. Fluff with fork.

Meanwhile, heat cooking oil in large frying pan on medium-high. Add chicken and onion. Scramble-fry for 8 to 10 minutes until chicken is no longer pink.

Add next 7 ingredients. Stir. Cook for about 5 minutes, stirring occasionally, until coleslaw is tender-crisp.

Add peaches. Cook and stir for about 1 minute until heated through. Remove from heat. Add yogurt. Stir. Serve over rice. Serves 4.

*1 serving: 732 Calories; 22.9 g Total Fat (2.3 g Mono, 1.3 g Poly, 0.5 g Sat); 1 mg Cholesterol; 103 g Carbohydrate; 5 g Fibre; 29 g Protein; 915 mg Sodium*

# Chicken Tofu Stir-Fry

*This sweet-and-sour, spicy stir-fry comes together in a snap.*
*Using ground chicken in stir-fries cuts down the prep time, and tofu is a great*
*addition to spicy dishes because it takes on the flavour of the ingredients*
*it is cooked with—and it counts as extra protein.*

| | | |
|---|---|---|
| Cooking oil | 2 tsp. | 10 mL |
| Chopped onion | 1 cup | 250 mL |
| Lean ground chicken | 1/2 lb. | 225 g |
| Garlic cloves, minced | 2 | 2 |
| (or 1/2 tsp., 2 mL, powder) | | |
| Chopped red pepper | 1 cup | 250 mL |
| Chopped yellow pepper | 1 cup | 250 mL |
| Soy sauce | 3 tbsp. | 50 mL |
| Brown sugar, packed | 2 tbsp. | 30 mL |
| Lime juice | 2 tbsp. | 30 mL |
| Sweet chili sauce | 2 tbsp. | 30 mL |
| Pepper | 1/4 tsp. | 1 mL |
| Diced firm tofu | 2 cups | 500 mL |

Heat cooking oil in large frying pan on medium-high. Add next 3 ingredients. Scramble-fry for 3 to 5 minutes until chicken is no longer pink.

Add next 7 ingredients. Stir. Cook, covered, for 2 to 4 minutes until peppers are tender-crisp.

Add tofu. Heat and stir for about 1 minute until heated through.
Makes about 4 1/2 cups (1.1 L).

*1 cup (250 mL): 239 Calories; 11.0 g Total Fat (1.6 g Mono, 1.8 g Poly, 0.5 g Sat); 0 mg Cholesterol; 18 g Carbohydrate; 2 g Fibre; 18 g Protein; 629 mg Sodium*

# Chicken Mole

*No need to go underground in search of an earthy chicken stew! Mole (pronounced MOH-lay) is a traditional spicy Mexican sauce that contains just enough cocoa to make it unique. You'll save time by preparing the ingredients for the sauce while the chicken cooks.*

| | | |
|---|---|---|
| Cooking oil | 1 tbsp. | 15 mL |
| Boneless, skinless chicken thighs, cut into 1 inch (2.5 cm) pieces | 1 lb. | 454 g |
| Chopped onion | 1 cup | 250 mL |
| Salt | 1/4 tsp. | 1 mL |
| Cayenne pepper | 1/4 tsp. | 1 mL |
| Can of tomato sauce | 7 1/2 oz. | 213 mL |
| Barbecue sauce | 1/2 cup | 125 mL |
| Water | 1/4 cup | 60 mL |
| Brown sugar, packed | 2 tbsp. | 30 mL |
| Cocoa, sifted if lumpy | 2 tbsp. | 30 mL |
| Dark raisins | 2 tbsp. | 30 mL |
| Peanut butter | 2 tbsp. | 30 mL |
| Chili powder | 1 tsp. | 5 mL |
| Garlic powder | 1/4 tsp. | 1 mL |
| Ground cinnamon | 1/4 tsp. | 1 mL |

Heat cooking oil in large frying pan on medium-high. Add next 4 ingredients. Cook for about 5 minutes, stirring occasionally, until chicken is no longer pink inside.

Add remaining 10 ingredients. Stir. Reduce heat to medium-low. Cook, covered, for about 10 minutes, stirring occasionally, until chicken is tender. Makes about 3 1/2 cups (875 mL).

*1 cup (250 mL): 398 Calories; 18.8 g Total Fat (8.3 g Mono, 4.9 g Poly, 4.0 g Sat); 87 mg Cholesterol; 31 g Carbohydrate; 6 g Fibre; 29 g Protein; 936 mg Sodium*

# Chicken Picadillo

*A Spanish favourite, picadillo (pronounced pee-kah-DEE-yoh) makes great use of common kitchen spices. This recipe may look long but it comes together quite quickly.*

| | | |
|---|---|---|
| Boneless, skinless chicken breast halves | 1 lb. | 454 g |
| Salt | 1/4 tsp. | 1 mL |
| Pepper | 1/8 tsp. | 0.5 mL |
| Ground cumin | 1 tsp. | 5 mL |
| Dried basil | 1/2 tsp. | 2 mL |
| Dried oregano | 1/2 tsp. | 2 mL |
| Garlic powder | 1/4 tsp. | 1 mL |
| Ground cinnamon | 1/4 tsp. | 1 mL |
| Salt | 1/4 tsp. | 1 mL |
| Olive (or cooking) oil | 2 tbsp. | 30 mL |
| Chopped onion | 1/4 cup | 60 mL |
| Tomato paste (see Coach, page 79) | 1 tbsp. | 15 mL |
| Dry (or alcohol-free) red wine | 1/4 cup | 60 mL |
| Can of diced tomatoes (with juice) | 14 oz. | 398 mL |
| Sliced green olives | 1/2 cup | 125 mL |
| Brown sugar, packed | 1 tbsp. | 15 mL |

Cut chicken crosswise into 3/4 inch (2 cm) strips. Sprinkle with salt and pepper.

Combine next 6 ingredients in small cup. Set aside.

Heat olive oil in large frying pan on medium-high. Cook chicken in 2 batches, for about 2 minutes per batch, stirring occasionally, until starting to brown. Transfer to plate. Cover to keep warm.

Add onion to same frying pan. Cook for about 5 minutes, stirring often, until softened.

Add tomato paste and spice mixture. Heat and stir for about 1 minute until fragrant. Add wine. Heat and stir for about 1 minute, scraping any brown bits from bottom of pan, until mixture resembles paste.

*(continued on next page)*

Add remaining 3 ingredients and chicken. Stir. Reduce heat to medium-low. Cook, covered, for about 5 minutes until chicken is no longer pink inside. Makes about 4 cups (1 L).

*1 cup (250 mL): 360 Calories; 15.4 g Total Fat (9.3 g Mono, 2.0 g Poly, 2.8 g Sat); 103 mg Cholesterol; 11 g Carbohydrate; 2 g Fibre; 40 g Protein; 1217 mg Sodium*

Pictured on page 54.

COACH

Slicing the chicken breast at a 45° angle will allow it to cook quickly but still remain tender.

# Chi-Chi Chicken Fingers

*This kiddie-favourite gets glammed up with a hint of lime.*

| | | |
|---|---|---|
| **Boneless, skinless chicken breast halves** | 1 lb. | 454 g |
| **Cornflake crumbs** | 1 cup | 250 mL |
| **Grated lime zest** | 1 tbsp. | 15 mL |
| **Granulated sugar** | 1 tsp. | 5 mL |
| **Salt** | 1 1/2 tsp. | 7 mL |
| **Pepper** | 1/2 tsp. | 2 mL |
| **Lime juice** | 1/4 cup | 60 mL |
| **Cooking spray** | | |

Preheat oven to 425°F (220°C). Cut each chicken breast lengthwise into 4 or 5 strips.

Combine next 5 ingredients in small bowl. Transfer to plate.

Measure lime juice into small shallow bowl. Dip chicken into lime juice. Roll in crumb mixture until coated. Arrange on greased baking sheet with sides. Spray chicken with cooking spray. Bake for about 15 minutes until no longer pink inside. Serves 4.

*1 serving: 170 Calories; 3.5 g Total Fat (1.3 g Mono, 0.8 g Poly, 0.9 g Sat); 66 mg Cholesterol; 9 g Carbohydrate; trace Fibre; 25 g Protein; 980 mg Sodium*

# Easy Chicken Paprikash

*Prepare an easy bash with this delightful paprikash! This creamy, tomato-laden stew makes quite an elegant entree when served over buttered egg noodles.*

| | | |
|---|---|---|
| All-purpose flour | 1/4 cup | 60 mL |
| Paprika | 1 tbsp. | 15 mL |
| Salt | 1 tsp. | 5 mL |
| Boneless, skinless chicken breast halves, cut into 1 inch (2.5 cm) pieces | 1 lb. | 454 g |
| Cooking oil | 1 tbsp. | 15 mL |
| Cooking oil | 2 tsp. | 10 mL |
| Chopped green pepper | 1 cup | 250 mL |
| Chopped onion | 1 cup | 250 mL |
| Can of diced tomatoes (with juice) | 14 oz. | 398 mL |
| Prepared chicken broth | 1/2 cup | 125 mL |
| Apple juice | 2 tbsp. | 30 mL |
| Dried dillweed | 2 tsp. | 10 mL |
| Sour cream | 1/3 cup | 75 mL |

Combine first 3 ingredients in medium resealable freezer bag. Add chicken. Seal bag. Toss until coated.

Heat first amount of cooking oil in large frying pan on medium-high. Add chicken. Set aside any remaining flour mixture. Cook for about 5 minutes, turning at halftime, until browned. Transfer to plate. Cover to keep warm.

Add second amount of cooking oil to same frying pan. Reduce heat to medium. Add green pepper and onion. Cook for 2 to 4 minutes, stirring often, until vegetables are tender-crisp. Add chicken and reserved flour mixture. Stir.

Add next 4 ingredients. Stir. Bring to a boil. Reduce heat to medium-low. Simmer, covered, for about 5 minutes, stirring occasionally, until vegetables are softened and chicken is no longer pink inside.

Add sour cream. Stir. Makes about 5 cups (1.25 L).

*1 cup (250 mL): 239 Calories; 10.3 g Total Fat (4.5 g Mono, 2.2 g Poly, 2.9 g Sat); 59 mg Cholesterol; 15 g Carbohydrate; 1 g Fibre; 22 g Protein; 820 mg Sodium*

Pictured on page 107.

# Cajun Chicken Po' Boys

*Give your mouth a workout with these jaw-extending sandwiches filled with spicy chicken, creamy mayo and crisp lettuce. If you don't have a loaf of French bread, just use kaiser rolls instead.*

| | | |
|---|---|---|
| Cooking oil | 2 tsp. | 10 mL |
| Chicken breast cutlets (about 1 lb., 454 g) | 4 | 4 |
| Cajun seasoning | 2 tsp. | 10 mL |
| Mayonnaise | 1/3 cup | 75 mL |
| Honey Dijon mustard | 1 tbsp. | 15 mL |
| French bread loaf, halved horizontally | 1 | 1 |
| Medium tomato, thinly sliced | 1 | 1 |
| Shredded iceberg lettuce, lightly packed | 2 cups | 500 mL |

Heat cooking oil in large frying pan on medium-high. Add chicken. Sprinkle with seasoning. Cook for 3 to 4 minutes per side until no longer pink inside.

Meanwhile, combine mayonnaise and mustard in small cup. Spread evenly on cut sides of bread.

Arrange tomato over mayonnaise mixture on bottom half of loaf. Arrange chicken over tomato.

Top with lettuce. Place top half of loaf, mayonnaise-side down, over lettuce. Cut loaf into 4 equal portions (see Coach, below). Makes 4 sandwiches.

*1 sandwich: 514 Calories; 34.2 g Total Fat (15.2 g Mono, 8.6 g Poly, 6.5 g Sat); 110 mg Cholesterol; 24 g Carbohydrate; 2 g Fibre; 26 g Protein; 1154 mg Sodium*

Pictured on page 107.

COACH — To keep your Po' Boy (and any other big sandwich, for that matter) from falling apart when you cut it, put four toothpicks, spaced evenly apart, into the top half of the loaf to prevent the chicken and bread from shifting.

# Chic Chicken Chili

*This home-on-the-range special is made chic with the addition of a subtle citrus flavour. This tastes just as good with ground turkey, and you can up the heat factor by adding a can of diced green chilies (4 oz., 113 g).*

| | | |
|---|---|---|
| Cooking oil | 1 tsp. | 5 mL |
| Lean ground chicken | 1 lb. | 454 g |
| Chopped onion | 1 cup | 250 mL |
| Garlic clove, minced | 1 | 1 |
| (or 1/4 tsp., 1 mL, powder) | | |
| Can of diced tomatoes (with juice) | 28 oz. | 796 mL |
| Can of black beans, rinsed and drained | 19 oz. | 540 mL |
| Can of sliced jalapeño peppers, drained | 4 oz. | 114 mL |
| (see Coach, page 75) | | |
| Orange juice | 1/4 cup | 60 mL |
| Brown sugar, packed | 1 tbsp. | 15 mL |
| Chili powder | 1 tsp. | 5 mL |
| Grated orange zest | 1 tsp. | 5 mL |

Heat cooking oil in large frying pan on medium-high. Add next 3 ingredients. Scramble-fry for 8 to 10 minutes until chicken is no longer pink and onion is softened.

Add remaining 7 ingredients. Bring to a boil. Reduce heat to medium-low. Simmer, covered, for 10 minutes to blend flavours. Makes about 6 1/2 cups (1.6 L).

*1 cup (250 mL): 238 Calories; 10.4 g Total Fat (0.4 g Mono, 0.3 g Poly, 0.1 g Sat); 0 mg Cholesterol; 23 g Carbohydrate; 5 g Fibre; 17 g Protein; 1013 mg Sodium*

Pictured on page 107.

1. Cajun Chicken Po' Boys, page 105
2. Chic Chicken Chili, above
3. Easy Chicken Paprikash, page 104

Props courtesy of: Pier 1 Imports

# Honey Garlic Salmon

*Glazing is a great method of flavouring all sorts of meats with a sweet coating. The simple flavours of honey and garlic go well with salmon.*

| | | |
|---|---|---|
| Brown sugar, packed | 2 tbsp. | 30 mL |
| Liquid honey | 2 tbsp. | 30 mL |
| Soy sauce | 1 tbsp. | 15 mL |
| Cornstarch | 2 tsp. | 10 mL |
| Garlic cloves, minced | 2 | 2 |
| (or 1/2 tsp., 2 mL, powder) | | |
| Finely grated gingerroot | 1 tsp. | 5 mL |
| (or 1/4 tsp., 1 mL, ground ginger) | | |
| Chili paste (sambal oelek), optional | 1 tsp. | 5 mL |
| Fresh (or frozen, thawed) | 4 | 4 |
| salmon fillets, skin removed | | |
| (4 – 5 oz., 113 – 140 g, each) | | |

Preheat oven to 400°F (205°C). Combine first 7 ingredients in small bowl.

Arrange fillets on baking sheet with sides, lined with greased foil. Spread honey mixture evenly over fillets. Bake for 10 to 15 minutes until fish flakes easily when tested with fork. Serves 4.

*1 serving: 761 Calories; 40.1 g Total Fat (17.2 g Mono, 8.0 g Poly, 9.6 g Sat); 254 mg Cholesterol; 17 g Carbohydrate; trace Fibre; 77 g Protein; 407 mg Sodium*

Pictured on page 108.

1. Seafood Tagine, page 112
2. Honey Garlic Salmon, above
3. Dill-icious Poached Salmon, page 110

Props courtesy of: Pier 1 Imports

# Dill-icious Poached Salmon

*Poaching is an easy, greaseless cooking method that results in moist and tender fish. The fish is gently cooked, just below the boiling point, in hot liquid.*

| | | |
|---|---|---|
| Water | 2 1/2 cups | 625 mL |
| Dry (or alcohol-free) white wine | 1/2 cup | 125 mL |
| Prepared chicken broth | 1/2 cup | 125 mL |
| Medium lemon, sliced | 1 | 1 |
| Finely chopped onion | 1/3 cup | 75 mL |
| Coarsely chopped fresh dill | 2 tbsp. | 30 mL |
| (or 1 1/2 tsp., 7 mL, dried) | | |
| Bay leaf, broken in half | 1 | 1 |
| Pepper | 1/4 tsp. | 1 mL |
| Salmon steaks | 4 | 4 |
| Butter (or hard margarine) | 2 tbsp. | 30 mL |
| All-purpose flour | 2 tbsp. | 30 mL |
| Milk | 1/2 cup | 125 mL |
| Chopped fresh dill | 1 tbsp. | 15 mL |
| (or 3/4 tsp., 4 mL, dried) | | |
| Salt | 1/4 tsp. | 1 mL |

Chopped fresh dill, for garnish

Combine first 8 ingredients in large frying pan. Bring to a boil. Reduce heat to low.

Place salmon in poaching liquid. Cook, covered, for about 8 minutes until fish flakes easily when tested with fork. Transfer salmon to serving plate. Cover to keep warm. Reserve 1 cup (250 mL) poaching liquid. Discard lemon slices, bay leaf and remaining poaching liquid.

Meanwhile, melt butter in medium saucepan on medium. Add flour. Heat and stir for 1 minute.

Slowly add milk, stirring constantly with whisk, until smooth. Heat and stir until boiling and thickened. Add reserved poaching liquid. Cook for 2 minutes, stirring occasionally, to blend flavours.

Add dill and salt. Stir. Pour over salmon.

Garnish with dill. Serves 4.

*(continued on next page)*

*1 serving:* 778 Calories; 46.2 g Total Fat (18.8 g Mono, 8.2 g Poly, 13.4 g Sat); 270 mg Cholesterol; 5 g Carbohydrate; trace Fibre; 79 g Protein; 447 mg Sodium

Pictured on page 108.

---

# Artichoke Salmon

*Red pepper and artichoke add a lively flavour to subtle salmon.*

| | | |
|---|---|---|
| Can of artichoke hearts, drained | 14 oz. | 398 mL |
| Grated Parmesan cheese | 3 tbsp. | 50 mL |
| Olive (or cooking) oil | 3 tbsp. | 50 mL |
| Dried oregano | 1/2 tsp. | 2 mL |
| Pepper | 1/4 tsp. | 1 mL |
| Finely chopped roasted red pepper | 1/4 cup | 60 mL |
| Fresh (or frozen, thawed) salmon fillets, skin removed (4 – 5 oz., 113 – 140 g, each) | 4 | 4 |

Preheat broiler. Put first 5 ingredients into blender or food processor. Process with on/off motion until coarsely chopped. Transfer to small bowl.

Add red pepper. Stir.

Arrange fillets on greased baking sheet with sides. Spread artichoke mixture over fillets. Broil on top rack in oven for about 8 minutes until fish flakes easily when tested with fork and top is starting to brown. Serves 4.

*1 serving:* 930 Calories; 57.2 g Total Fat (26.8 g Mono, 9.0 g Poly, 15.3 g Sat); 272 mg Cholesterol; 8 g Carbohydrate; 1 g Fibre; 89 g Protein; 906 mg Sodium

# Seafood Tagine

*Tagine is a Moroccan stew but the name also refers to the type of pot the stew is cooked in. Don't worry though, all you need to cook this sweet, fruity tagine is a saucepan. Serve on couscous or rice.*

| | | |
|---|---|---|
| Cooking oil | 1 tsp. | 5 mL |
| Chopped onion | 1 cup | 250 mL |
| Chopped red pepper | 1 cup | 250 mL |
| Finely grated gingerroot | 2 tsp. | 10 mL |
| (or 1/2 tsp., 2 mL, ground ginger) | | |
| Garlic cloves, minced | 2 | 2 |
| (or 1/2 tsp., 2 mL, powder) | | |
| Ground cinnamon | 1/2 tsp. | 2 mL |
| Salt | 1/2 tsp. | 2 mL |
| Pepper | 1/2 tsp. | 2 mL |
| Ground cumin | 1/4 tsp. | 1 mL |
| All-purpose flour | 1 tbsp. | 15 mL |
| Prepared vegetable broth | 1 cup | 250 mL |
| Dry (or alcohol-free) white wine | 1/2 cup | 125 mL |
| Chopped dried apricot | 1/4 cup | 60 mL |
| Raisins | 1/4 cup | 60 mL |
| Liquid honey | 2 tbsp. | 30 mL |
| Lemon juice | 2 tsp. | 10 mL |
| Frozen, uncooked medium shrimp | 1/2 lb. | 225 g |
| (peeled and deveined), thawed | | |
| Fresh (or frozen, thawed) small bay scallops | 6 oz. | 170 g |

Heat cooking oil in medium saucepan on medium. Add next 8 ingredients. Cook for about 5 minutes, stirring occasionally, until onion starts to soften.

Add flour. Heat and stir for 1 minute.

Slowly add broth, stirring constantly, until smooth. Add next 5 ingredients. Heat and stir until boiling and thickened. Reduce heat to medium-low. Simmer, uncovered, for 5 minutes, stirring constantly, to blend flavours.

Add shrimp and scallops. Stir. Cook for about 2 minutes until shrimp turn pink and scallops are opaque. Makes about 4 cups (1 L).

*1 cup (250 mL): 259 Calories; 2.8 g Total Fat (0.8 g Mono, 0.9 g Poly, 0.4 g Sat); 100 mg Cholesterol; 34 g Carbohydrate; 3 g Fibre; 21 g Protein; 571 mg Sodium*

Pictured on page 108.

# Rum Runner Shrimp

*The rum and sweet pineapple in this shrimp dish will leave*
*you thinking easy, breezy tropical thoughts. (Cooking with alcohol*
*will flavour dishes with the essence of that particular liquor—most*
*of the time the actual alcohol content is evaporated.)*

| | | |
|---|---|---|
| Butter (or hard margarine) | 2 tbsp. | 30 mL |
| Garlic cloves, minced | 2 | 2 |
| (or 1/2 tsp., 2 mL, powder) | | |
| Frozen, uncooked large shrimp (peeled and deveined), thawed | 1 lb. | 454 g |
| Reserved pineapple juice | 1/3 cup | 75 mL |
| Dark (navy) rum | 3 tbsp. | 50 mL |
| Lime juice | 3 tbsp. | 50 mL |
| Brown sugar, packed | 1 tbsp. | 15 mL |
| Cornstarch | 1 tsp. | 5 mL |
| Grated lime zest | 1/2 tsp. | 2 mL |
| Chili paste (sambal oelek) | 1/4 tsp. | 1 mL |
| Can of pineapple chunks, drained and juice reserved | 14 oz. | 398 mL |
| Chopped green onion | 1/4 cup | 60 mL |

Melt butter in large frying pan on medium. Add garlic. Heat and stir
for about 1 minute until fragrant. Add shrimp. Cook for about 3 minutes,
stirring often, until shrimp start to turn pink. Transfer to plate using slotted
spoon. Cover to keep warm.

Combine next 7 ingredients in small bowl. Add to same frying pan.
Bring to a boil on medium. Cook for about 2 minutes, stirring constantly,
until sauce starts to thicken.

Add pineapple and shrimp. Cook for about 2 minutes, stirring occasionally,
until heated through.

Sprinkle green onion over top. Makes about 4 cups (1 L).

*1 cup (250 mL): 287 Calories; 7.8 g Total Fat (1.8 g Mono, 1.0 g Poly, 4.0 g Sat);*
*187 mg Cholesterol; 25 g Carbohydrate; 1 g Fibre; 24 g Protein; 218 mg Sodium*

# Garlic Clam Linguine

*We're not going to clam up about this one. How often do you get served
a clam entree at someone's home? This is a neat dinner treat.
And if you're in a real big rush, use 1/4 cup (60 mL)
of real bacon bits in place of the diced bacon and substitute
about 1 tsp. (5 mL) olive oil for the bacon drippings.*

| | | |
|---|---|---|
| Water | 12 cups | 3 L |
| Salt | 1 1/2 tsp. | 7 mL |
| Linguine | 14 oz. | 395 g |
| Olive oil | 1 tbsp. | 15 mL |
| Bacon slices, diced | 3 | 3 |
| Finely chopped onion | 1/3 cup | 75 mL |
| Garlic cloves, minced | 3 | 3 |
| Can of whole baby clams (with juice) | 5 oz. | 142 g |
| Dry (or alcohol-free) white wine | 1/2 cup | 125 mL |
| Pepper | 1/2 tsp. | 2 mL |
| Chopped fresh parsley | 1/4 cup | 60 mL |
| Grated Parmesan cheese | 2 tbsp. | 30 mL |
| Chopped fresh basil | 1 tbsp. | 15 mL |

Combine water and salt in Dutch oven or large pot. Bring to a boil.
Add pasta. Boil, uncovered, for about 10 minutes, stirring occasionally,
until tender but firm. Drain, reserving 1/2 cup (125 mL) cooking water.
Return to same pot. Add olive oil. Toss until coated. Cover to keep warm.

Meanwhile, cook bacon in large frying pan on medium for about
4 minutes until crisp.

Add onion and garlic. Cook for about 2 minutes, stirring often, until onion
is softened.

Add next 3 ingredients. Stir. Bring to a boil on medium. Cook for 2 minutes
to blend flavours. Add to pasta. Toss.

Sprinkle with remaining 3 ingredients. Toss, adding reserved cooking water
a little at a time, if needed, to moisten. Makes about 6 cups (1.5 L).

*1 cup (250 mL):* *402 Calories; 12.0 g Total Fat (6.3 g Mono, 1.2 g Poly, 5.7 g Sat);
34 mg Cholesterol; 53 g Carbohydrate; 2 g Fibre; 18 g Protein; 437 mg Sodium*

# Fish Tacos

*If you travel down Mexico way, you'll find that fish tacos are very popular. Paired with a spicy avocado, mango and tomato salsa, they're well worth it.*

| | | |
|---|---|---|
| Haddock fillets, any small bones removed | 1 lb. | 454 g |
| Salt, sprinkle | | |
| Pepper, sprinkle | | |
| Hard taco shells | 8 | 8 |
| Diced ripe avocado | 1 cup | 250 mL |
| Diced tomato | 2/3 cup | 150 mL |
| Mango chutney, larger pieces chopped | 1/3 cup | 75 mL |
| Lime juice | 1 tbsp. | 15 mL |
| Dried crushed chilies | 1/2 tsp. | 2 mL |

Preheat oven to 400°F (205°C). Arrange fillets on greased baking sheet with sides. Sprinkle with salt and pepper. Bake for about 8 minutes until fish flakes easily when tested with fork. Cut into bite-sized pieces.

Meanwhile, arrange taco shells on separate ungreased baking sheet. Place in hot oven for about 5 minutes until warm.

Combine remaining 5 ingredients in medium bowl. Arrange fish in taco shells. Spoon avocado mixture over top. Makes 8 tacos.

*1 taco: 160 Calories; 6.6 g Total Fat (1.9 g Mono, 0.5 g Poly, 1.2 g Sat); 32 mg Cholesterol; 14 g Carbohydrate; 2 g Fibre; 12 g Protein; 190 mg Sodium*

# Thoroughly Modern Chili

*Forget everything you know about chili—this modern take has scallops, clams, lentils and a mild heat from chipotle peppers. Serve with rolls or Feta Polenta Muffins, page 74.*

| | | |
|---|---|---|
| Cooking oil | 2 tsp. | 10 mL |
| Chopped onion | 1 cup | 250 mL |
| Chopped red pepper | 1 cup | 250 mL |
| Garlic cloves, minced | 2 | 2 |
| (or 1/2 tsp., 2 mL, powder) | | |
| Can of lentils, rinsed and drained | 19 oz. | 540 mL |
| Tomato sauce | 2 cups | 500 mL |
| Dry (or alcohol-free) white wine | 1/2 cup | 125 mL |
| Chili powder | 1 tsp. | 5 mL |
| Finely chopped chipotle peppers | 1 tsp. | 5 mL |
| in adobo sauce (see Coach, page 133) | | |
| Ground cumin | 1/2 tsp. | 2 mL |
| Salt | 1/2 tsp. | 2 mL |
| Fresh (or frozen, thawed) small bay scallops | 1/2 lb. | 225 g |
| Can of diced tomatoes, drained | 14 oz. | 398 mL |
| Can of whole baby clams, drained | 5 oz. | 142 g |
| Lime juice | 1 tbsp. | 15 mL |
| Chopped fresh cilantro or parsley | 2 tsp. | 10 mL |

Heat cooking oil in large saucepan on medium-high. Add next 3 ingredients. Cook for about 5 minutes, stirring occasionally, until onion is softened.

Add next 7 ingredients. Stir. Bring to a boil. Reduce heat to medium. Boil gently, uncovered, for about 5 minutes until thickened.

Add scallops. Stir. Cook for about 3 minutes until scallops are opaque.

Add remaining 4 ingredients. Heat and stir for 1 minute. Makes about 8 cups (2 L).

*1 cup (250 mL): 160 Calories; 2.2 g Total Fat (0.7 g Mono, 0.5 g Poly, 0.3 g Sat); 24 mg Cholesterol; 20 g Carbohydrate; 7 g Fibre; 13 g Protein; 857 mg Sodium*

Pictured on page 89.

# Cioppino

*Cioppino (pronounced chuh-PEE-noh) is a hearty tomato and seafood soup. Our version is so hearty, you can actually serve it over pasta. Or eat it the traditional way with some crusty rolls.*

| | | |
|---|---|---|
| Cooking oil | 1 tbsp. | 15 mL |
| Chopped onion | 1 1/2 cups | 375 mL |
| Sliced fresh white mushrooms | 1 1/2 cups | 375 mL |
| Chopped red pepper | 1 cup | 250 mL |
| Garlic cloves, minced (or 1/2 tsp., 2 mL, powder) | 2 | 2 |
| Dry (or alcohol-free) white wine | 1/4 cup | 60 mL |
| Can of chunky tomatoes (with juice) | 19 oz. | 540 mL |
| Tomato paste (see Coach, page 79) | 2 tbsp. | 30 mL |
| Granulated sugar | 1 tsp. | 5 mL |
| Italian seasoning | 1 tsp. | 5 mL |
| Salt | 1/4 tsp. | 1 mL |
| Fresh (or frozen, thawed) salmon fillets, skin removed, cut into 1 inch (2.5 cm) cubes | 1/2 lb. | 225 g |
| Fresh (or frozen, thawed) small bay scallops | 1/2 lb. | 225 g |
| Frozen, uncooked medium shrimp (peeled and deveined), thawed | 1/2 lb. | 225 g |

Heat cooking oil in large frying pan on medium-high. Add next 4 ingredients. Cook for about 5 minutes, stirring occasionally, until onion is softened.

Add wine. Stir. Add next 5 ingredients. Stir. Bring to a boil. Reduce heat to medium. Boil gently, uncovered, for about 5 minutes until slightly thickened.

Add remaining 3 ingredients. Stir. Boil gently, uncovered, for about 5 minutes, stirring occasionally, until fish flakes easily when tested with fork, shrimp turn pink and scallops are opaque. Makes about 7 cups (1.75 L).

*1 cup (250 mL): 211 Calories; 6.3 g Total Fat (2.7 g Mono, 1.6 g Poly, 1.1 g Sat); 81 mg Cholesterol; 16 g Carbohydrate; 2 g Fibre; 21 g Protein; 547 mg Sodium*

COACH

Be careful not to overcook seafood. Overcooking makes it too tough and chewy.

# Honey Pecan Pasta

*Taste the unexpected in this stylish pesto-dressed*
*linguine with toasted honey pecans.*

| | | |
|---|---|---|
| Water | 8 cups | 2 L |
| Salt | 1 tsp. | 5 mL |
| Linguine | 8 oz. | 225 g |
| Chopped pecans | 1 cup | 250 mL |
| Butter (or hard margarine) | 1 tbsp. | 15 mL |
| Honey | 2 tbsp. | 30 mL |
| Basil pesto | 1/3 cup | 75 mL |
| Chopped fresh parsley | 2 tbsp. | 30 mL |
| Lemon juice | 1 tbsp. | 15 mL |
| Salt | 1/4 tsp. | 1 mL |
| Pepper | 1/4 tsp. | 1 mL |

Combine water and salt in large saucepan or Dutch oven. Bring to a boil. Add pasta. Boil, uncovered, for about 10 minutes, stirring occasionally, until tender but firm. Drain. Return to same pot. Cover to keep warm.

Meanwhile, heat large frying pan on medium. Add pecans. Cook for about 5 minutes, stirring occasionally, until toasted. Add butter. Heat and stir until melted. Add honey. Stir until coated. Add to pasta. Toss.

Add remaining 5 ingredients. Toss until coated. Makes about 4 cups (1 L).

*1 cup (250 mL): 533 Calories; 31.0 g Total Fat (12.7 g Mono, 6.5 g Poly, 4.8 g Sat); 10 mg Cholesterol; 56 g Carbohydrate; 5 g Fibre; 12 g Protein; 306 mg Sodium*

Pictured on page 125.

Parsley can be quite a problem—recipes only call for small amounts, yet it's sold in bountiful bundles. What are you supposed to do with the leftover parsley? Wash and chop what you don't think you'll be using in the next few days, and fill an ice cube tray 3/4 full of parsley and cover with water. Then freeze to have individual parsley cubes at your disposal. When you need parsley just let the ice cube thaw and blot the leaves. This trick works great with many fresh herbs.

# Sweet Potato Lentil Stew

*Sweet potatoes add an unexpected flavour to this delightful stew—and unlike traditional stews, this one doesn't need to simmer for hours on end.*

| | | |
|---|---|---|
| Cooking oil | 1 tbsp. | 15 mL |
| Chopped eggplant (with peel) | 2 cups | 500 mL |
| Chopped onion | 2 cups | 500 mL |
| Sliced celery | 1 cup | 250 mL |
| Garlic clove, minced | 1 | 1 |
| (or 1/4 tsp., 1 mL, powder) | | |
| Dried oregano | 1 tsp. | 5 mL |
| Granulated sugar | 1 tsp. | 5 mL |
| Ground cumin | 1 tsp. | 5 mL |
| Salt | 1/2 tsp. | 2 mL |
| Chili powder | 1/4 tsp. | 1 mL |
| Can of lentils, rinsed and drained | 19 oz. | 540 mL |
| Can of sweet potatoes, drained and chopped | 19 oz. | 540 mL |
| Can of diced tomatoes (with juice) | 14 oz. | 398 mL |
| Prepared vegetable broth | 1 cup | 250 mL |

Heat cooking oil in large frying pan on medium-high. Add next 4 ingredients. Cook for about 5 minutes, stirring often, until onion is softened.

Add next 5 ingredients. Heat and stir for about 1 minute until fragrant.

Add remaining 4 ingredients. Stir. Bring to a boil. Reduce heat to medium. Cook, covered, for 10 minutes, stirring occasionally, to blend flavours. Makes about 6 cups (1.5 L).

*1 cup (250 mL): 254 Calories; 3.0 g Total Fat (1.4 g Mono, 0.9 g Poly, 0.3 g Sat); 0 mg Cholesterol; 50 g Carbohydrate; 14 g Fibre; 9 g Protein; 613 mg Sodium*

# Florentine Mushrooms

*If a dish is served florentine, expect there to be spinach and cheese—
and, in this case, a flashy presentation.*

| | | |
|---|---|---|
| Portobello mushrooms (about 4 inch, 10 cm, diameter), stems removed | 4 | 4 |
| Italian dressing | 2 tbsp. | 30 mL |
| Cooking oil | 1 tsp. | 5 mL |
| Box of frozen chopped spinach, thawed and squeezed dry | 10 oz. | 300 g |
| Large eggs, fork-beaten | 2 | 2 |
| Sun-dried tomato pesto | 1/4 cup | 60 mL |
| Pepper | 3/4 tsp. | 4 mL |
| Grated mozzarella cheese | 1 cup | 250 mL |
| Chopped green onion | 1/4 cup | 60 mL |
| Fine dry bread crumbs | 1/4 cup | 60 mL |
| Grated Parmesan cheese | 1/4 cup | 60 mL |

Preheat oven to 400°F (205°C). Using small spoon, remove and discard gills from mushroom caps. Brush dressing on both sides of mushrooms. Place in greased 9 × 13 inch (22 × 33 cm) baking dish. Bake for about 8 minutes until starting to soften.

Meanwhile, heat cooking oil in large frying pan on medium. Add spinach. Cook and stir for about 3 minutes until softened.

Add next 3 ingredients. Cook and stir for about 1 minute until egg starts to set. Remove from heat.

Add next 3 ingredients. Stir until just combined. Spoon egg mixture into mushrooms.

Sprinkle Parmesan cheese over top. Bake for about 10 minutes until cheese is melted and golden. Makes 4 stuffed mushrooms.

*1 stuffed mushroom: 402 Calories; 24.9 g Total Fat (9.6 g Mono, 3.1 g Poly, 11.0 g Sat); 145 mg Cholesterol; 19 g Carbohydrate; 5 g Fibre; 28 g Protein; 1105 mg Sodium*

Mains — Meatless

# Browned Butter Fettuccine

*The simplicity of this dish is what makes it so appealing. With toasted pine nuts and a sprinkling of feta, it's perfect for those nights when you want your life, and your food, simplified.*

| | | |
|---|---|---|
| Water | 8 cups | 2 L |
| Salt | 1 tsp. | 5 mL |
| Fettuccine | 8 oz. | 225 g |
| Snow peas, trimmed and halved | 1 cup | 250 mL |
| Butter | 1/4 cup | 60 mL |
| Pine nuts | 1/2 cup | 125 mL |
| Salt | 1/8 tsp. | 0.5 mL |
| Crumbled feta cheese | 3/4 cup | 175 mL |

Combine water and salt in large saucepan or Dutch oven. Bring to a boil. Add fettuccine. Boil, uncovered, for 8 minutes, stirring occasionally.

Add peas. Cook for 1 to 2 minutes until fettuccine is tender but firm and peas are tender-crisp. Drain. Return to same pot. Cover to keep warm.

Meanwhile, heat butter in small frying pan on medium until melted and bubbling. Add pine nuts. Heat and stir for about 4 minutes until butter is browned and pine nuts are golden. Add to fettuccine. Add salt. Toss until coated.

Sprinkle cheese over top. Makes about 4 cups (1 L).

*1 cup (250 mL): 511 Calories; 28.5 g Total Fat (8.1 g Mono, 4.9 g Poly, 13.3 g Sat); 56 mg Cholesterol; 49 g Carbohydrate; 5 g Fibre; 18 g Protein; 483 mg Sodium*

If a recipe calls for butter, don't think you can automatically substitute margarine and get the same results. Butter browns easier and, sometimes, just performs better.

# Swift Veggie Stir-Fry

*Stir-fries are well-loved and cook up in a flash—it's the chopping that eats up your time. If you're rushed, use pre-cut or frozen veggies.*

| | | |
|---|---|---|
| Prepared vegetable broth | 1/2 cup | 125 mL |
| Hoisin sauce | 3 tbsp. | 50 mL |
| Rice vinegar | 2 tbsp. | 30 mL |
| Cornstarch | 1 tbsp. | 15 mL |
| Cooking oil | 1 tbsp. | 15 mL |
| Coleslaw mix | 2 cups | 500 mL |
| Sliced carrot | 1 cup | 250 mL |
| Sliced onion | 1 cup | 250 mL |
| Garlic cloves, minced | 2 | 2 |
| (or 1/2 tsp., 2 mL, powder) | | |
| Finely grated gingerroot | 1 tsp. | 5 mL |
| (or 1/4 tsp., 1 mL, ground ginger) | | |
| Frozen Oriental mixed vegetables | 6 cups | 1.5 L |
| Chopped red pepper | 1 cup | 250 mL |
| Chopped dry-roasted peanuts (optional) | 1/4 cup | 60 mL |

Combine first 4 ingredients in small bowl.

Heat large frying pan or wok on medium-high until very hot. Add cooking oil. Add next 5 ingredients. Stir-fry for 3 minutes.

Add mixed vegetables and red pepper. Stir-fry for about 3 minutes until vegetables are tender-crisp. Stir cornstarch mixture. Add to vegetable mixture. Heat and stir for about 1 minute until boiling and thickened.

Sprinkle with peanuts. Makes about 5 cups (1.25 L).

*1 cup (250 mL): 198 Calories; 5.1 g Total Fat (1.7 g Mono, 1.1 g Poly, 0.6 g Sat); 1 mg Cholesterol; 32 g Carbohydrate; 4 g Fibre; 6 g Protein; 905 mg Sodium*

Pictured on page 125.

COACH

Can't stand the smell of garlic on your hands? After you're done all the handling, rub used, wet coffee grounds between your hands and then rinse with water.

# Mediterranean Pizza

*You'll never be satisfied with delivery pizza again! Instead of throwing on a few green peppers and mushrooms and calling it vegetarian pizza, we pulled out all the stops—artichokes, sun-dried tomato, olives and feta!*

| | | |
|---|---|---|
| Prebaked pizza crust (12 inch, 30 cm, diameter) | 1 | 1 |
| Sun-dried tomato pesto | 1/4 cup | 60 mL |
| Grated mozzarella cheese | 3/4 cup | 175 mL |
| Jar of marinated artichoke hearts, drained, blotted dry and quartered | 6 oz. | 170 mL |
| Can of sliced black olives, drained | 4 1/2 oz. | 125 mL |
| Crumbled feta cheese | 3/4 cup | 175 mL |
| Dried crushed chilies | 1/2 tsp. | 2 mL |
| Chopped fresh basil | 3 tbsp. | 50 mL |

Preheat oven to 450°F (230°C). Place pizza crust on ungreased 12 inch (30 cm) pizza pan. Spread pesto evenly over crust. Sprinkle mozzarella cheese over top.

Sprinkle next 4 ingredients, in order given, over mozzarella cheese. Bake for 12 to 15 minutes until heated through and cheese is golden.

Sprinkle basil over top. Cuts into 8 wedges.

*1 wedge: 118 Calories; 7.5 g Total Fat (2.7 g Mono, 0.3 g Poly, 3.9 g Sat); 22 mg Cholesterol; 7 g Carbohydrate; 1 g Fibre; 6 g Protein; 508 mg Sodium*

# Vegetable Chili Pot

*This chili is proof positive that a vegetarian one-dish meal
can be just as filling as any meat-and-potatoes fare.*

| Cooking oil | 1 tbsp. | 15 mL |
|---|---|---|
| Chopped onion | 2 cups | 500 mL |
| Sliced fresh white mushrooms | 2 cups | 500 mL |
| Chopped green pepper | 1 cup | 250 mL |
| Can of black beans, rinsed and drained | 19 oz. | 540 mL |
| Tomato pasta sauce | 2 cups | 500 mL |
| Can of red kidney beans, rinsed and drained | 14 oz. | 398 mL |
| Can of stewed tomatoes, chopped | 14 oz. | 398 mL |
| Frozen kernel corn | 1 cup | 250 mL |
| Chili powder | 1 tbsp. | 15 mL |
| Ground cumin | 1 tsp. | 5 mL |
| Salt | 1/4 tsp. | 1 mL |
| Cayenne pepper | 1/4 tsp. | 1 mL |

Heat cooking oil in large saucepan or Dutch oven on medium-high.
Add next 3 ingredients. Cook, uncovered, for about 5 minutes, stirring
often, until onion is softened.

Add remaining 9 ingredients. Stir. Bring to a boil. Reduce heat to
medium-low. Simmer, covered, for 10 minutes, stirring occasionally,
to blend flavours. Makes about 9 cups (2.25 L).

*1 cup (250 mL): 156 Calories; 2.3 g Total Fat (1.0 g Mono, 0.6 g Poly, 0.2 g Sat); 0 mg Cholesterol;
30 g Carbohydrate; 8 g Fibre; 8 g Protein; 840 mg Sodium*

Pictured on page 125.

1. Swift Veggie Stir-Fry, page 122
2. Honey Pecan Pasta, page 118
3. Vegetable Chili Pot, above

Props courtesy of: Stokes

# Spiced Orange Ham Steaks

*With ham, it's all about the glaze. This sweet clove and cinnamon-scented glaze complements the smoky ham flavour perfectly.*

| | | |
|---|---|---|
| Brown sugar, packed | 1/4 cup | 60 mL |
| Frozen concentrated orange juice | 1/4 cup | 60 mL |
| Ground cinnamon | 1/8 tsp. | 0.5 mL |
| Ground cloves | 1/8 tsp. | 0.5 mL |
| Ham steaks (4 – 5 oz., 113 – 140 g, each) | 4 | 4 |

Combine first 4 ingredients in large frying pan. Heat and stir on medium for 2 to 3 minutes until sugar is dissolved and mixture starts to thicken.

Add ham. Cook for about 5 minutes, turning at halftime, until heated through and glazed. Serves 4.

*1 serving: 227 Calories; 5.2 g Total Fat (2.4 g Mono, 0.6 g Poly, 1.7 g Sat); 54 mg Cholesterol; 20 g Carbohydrate; trace Fibre; 24 g Protein; 1529 mg Sodium*

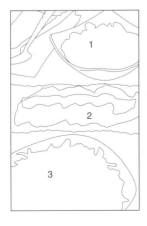

1. Hoisin Pork Stir-Fry, page 130
2. Balsamic Pork Chops, page 128
3. Orange Pork Stir-Fry, page 129

Props courtesy of: The Dazzling Gourmet
Winners Stores

# Balsamic Pork Chops

*Simple yet so satisfying. The sweet-and-tangy balsamic glaze enhances the natural flavours of these tender chops.*

| | | |
|---|---|---|
| Cooking oil | 2 tsp. | 10 mL |
| Bone-in pork chops, trimmed of fat | 4 | 4 |
| (5 – 6 oz., 140 – 170 g, each) | | |
| Salt | 1/4 tsp. | 1 mL |
| Pepper | 1/4 tsp. | 1 mL |
| Cooking oil | 1/2 tsp. | 2 mL |
| Finely chopped onion | 1/2 cup | 125 mL |
| Orange juice | 1/2 cup | 125 mL |
| Balsamic vinegar | 3 tbsp. | 50 mL |
| Brown sugar, packed | 3 tbsp. | 50 mL |
| Dijon mustard | 1 tsp. | 5 mL |

Heat first amount of cooking oil in large frying pan on medium-high. Sprinkle both sides of pork with salt and pepper. Add to frying pan. Cook for about 2 minutes per side until browned. Reduce heat to medium. Cook for about 5 minutes until desired doneness. Transfer to plate. Cover to keep warm.

Add second amount of cooking oil to same frying pan. Add onion. Cook for 2 to 4 minutes, stirring often, until onion is softened and starting to brown.

Add remaining 4 ingredients. Stir. Bring to a boil. Reduce heat to medium-low. Simmer, uncovered, for 8 to 10 minutes until slightly thickened. Serve with pork. Serves 4.

*1 serving: 288 Calories; 14.4 g Total Fat (6.8 g Mono, 1.8 g Poly, 4.4 g Sat); 61 mg Cholesterol; 17 g Carbohydrate; trace Fibre; 22 g Protein; 217 mg Sodium*

Pictured on page 126 and on back cover.

For medium doneness of pork the measured internal temperature should reach 160°F (70°C). If you don't have a meat thermometer (though we strongly suggest you should), make sure the pork is no longer pink inside and juices run clear.

# Orange Pork Stir-Fry

*This stir-fry is all about layering flavours. First, an initial hint of orange flavour. Second, a nice hit of chili heat. Attractive and colourful, this is an interesting and fun entree for your next dinner. Serious chili-heads can add double the amount of chili paste.*

| | | |
|---|---|---|
| Prepared chicken broth | 1/4 cup | 60 mL |
| Cornstarch | 1 tbsp. | 15 mL |
| Orange juice | 1/4 cup | 60 mL |
| Brown sugar, packed | 1 tbsp. | 15 mL |
| Soy sauce | 1 tbsp. | 15 mL |
| Finely grated gingerroot | 1 tsp. | 5 mL |
|    (or 1/4 tsp., 1 mL, ground ginger) | | |
| Grated orange zest | 1 tsp. | 5 mL |
| Chili paste (sambal oelek) | 1/2 tsp. | 2 mL |
| Cooking oil | 1 tbsp. | 15 mL |
| Pork tenderloin, trimmed of fat, cut in half | 1 lb. | 454 g |
|    lengthwise and cut crosswise into | | |
|    1/4 inch (6 mm) slices | | |
| Sliced red pepper | 1 cup | 250 mL |
| Thinly sliced onion | 1 cup | 250 mL |
| Fresh bean sprouts | 1 cup | 250 mL |
| Sliced green onion | 1/4 cup | 60 mL |

Stir broth into cornstarch in small cup. Add next 6 ingredients. Stir. Set aside.

Heat large frying pan or wok on medium-high until very hot. Add cooking oil. Add pork. Stir-fry for about 5 minutes until starting to brown.

Add red pepper and onion. Stir-fry for about 3 minutes until onion is tender-crisp. Stir cornstarch mixture. Add to pork mixture. Heat and stir for about 1 minute until boiling and thickened.

Add bean sprouts and green onion. Cook and stir until heated through. Makes about 4 cups (1 L).

*1 cup (250 mL): 276 Calories; 10.5 g Total Fat (4.8 g Mono, 1.8 g Poly, 2.7 g Sat); 78 mg Cholesterol; 18 g Carbohydrate; 2 g Fibre; 28 g Protein; 362 mg Sodium*

Pictured on page 126 and on back cover.

# Hoisin Pork Stir-Fry

*Pork is perfect in this sweet-and-spicy peanut stir-fry.*

| | | |
|---|---|---|
| Cooking oil | 1 tbsp. | 15 mL |
| Pork tenderloin, trimmed of fat and cut into 3/4 inch (2 cm) pieces | 1 lb. | 454 g |
| Sliced onion | 1 cup | 250 mL |
| Sliced red pepper | 1 cup | 250 mL |
| Can of sliced water chestnuts, drained | 8 oz. | 227 mL |
| Frozen peas | 3/4 cup | 175 mL |
| Hoisin sauce | 1/3 cup | 75 mL |
| Water | 2 tbsp. | 30 mL |
| Finely grated gingerroot (or 1/4 tsp., 1 mL, ground ginger) | 1 tsp. | 5 mL |
| Dried crushed chilies | 1/2 tsp. | 2 mL |
| Dry-roasted peanuts, chopped | 1/4 cup | 60 mL |

Heat large frying pan or wok on medium-high until very hot. Add cooking oil. Add pork. Stir-fry for 2 to 3 minutes until browned.

Add next 3 ingredients. Stir-fry for 2 to 3 minutes until vegetables are tender-crisp.

Add peas. Stir.

Combine next 4 ingredients in small cup. Add to pork mixture. Heat and stir for 2 minutes.

Sprinkle peanuts over top. Makes about 5 cups (1.25 L).

*1 cup (250 mL): 298 Calories; 12.7 g Total Fat (5.8 g Mono, 2.8 g Poly, 2.8 g Sat); 63 mg Cholesterol; 23 g Carbohydrate; 5 g Fibre; 24 g Protein; 345 mg Sodium*

Pictured on page 126 and on back cover.

Stir-fries cook up mighty quickly so have all your prepared ingredients at the ready before you start cooking. Start some rice cooking before you start prepping the stir-fry, or serve the stir-fry as a filling for big lettuce leaf wraps.

# Quick Pork Cassoulet

*This quick and tasty version of the classic French stew*
*makes great cold-weather fare.*

| | | |
|---|---|---|
| Cooking oil | 1 tsp. | 5 mL |
| Boneless fast-fry pork chops, trimmed of fat and cut into 6 pieces each | 1 lb. | 454 g |
| Seasoned salt | 1/2 tsp. | 2 mL |
| Cooking oil | 1 tsp. | 5 mL |
| Chopped carrot | 1 cup | 250 mL |
| Chopped onion | 1 cup | 250 mL |
| Chopped green pepper | 1/2 cup | 125 mL |
| Dried thyme | 1 tsp. | 5 mL |
| Garlic clove, minced (or 1/4 tsp., 1 mL, powder) | 1 | 1 |
| Granulated sugar | 1 tsp. | 5 mL |
| Pepper | 1/4 tsp. | 1 mL |
| Cans of mixed beans (19 oz., 540 mL, each), rinsed and drained | 2 | 2 |
| Can of diced tomatoes (with juice) | 14 oz. | 398 mL |
| Prepared chicken broth | 1/2 cup | 125 mL |

Heat first amount of cooking oil in Dutch oven on medium-high. Add pork. Sprinkle with seasoned salt. Cook, uncovered, for about 3 minutes, stirring occasionally, until starting to brown. Transfer to plate. Cover to keep warm.

Add second amount of cooking oil to same pot. Add next 7 ingredients. Cook for about 3 minutes, stirring often, until onion starts to soften.

Add remaining 3 ingredients and pork. Stir, scraping any brown bits from bottom of pan. Bring to a boil. Reduce heat to medium-low. Simmer, covered, for about 10 minutes until vegetables are tender. Makes about 7 cups (1.75 L).

*1 cup (250 mL): 259 Calories; 7.7 g Total Fat (3.2 g Mono, 0.9 g Poly, 2.2 g Sat); 34 mg Cholesterol; 30 g Carbohydrate; 7 g Fibre; 20 g Protein; 585 mg Sodium*

Pictured on page 143.

# Lamb Burgers

*Lots of rookie cooks stay away from lamb because they think it requires special cooking techniques. It doesn't! Working with ground lamb is just like working with ground beef—but it gives burgers a whole new flavour twist. You'll find frozen ground lamb in the freezer section of your grocery store.*

| | | |
|---|---|---|
| Fine dry bread crumbs | 1/4 cup | 60 mL |
| Steak sauce | 3 tbsp. | 50 mL |
| Chopped green onion | 2 tbsp. | 30 mL |
| Dijon mustard | 1 tbsp. | 15 mL |
| Garlic clove, minced | 1 | 1 |
| (or 1/4 tsp., 1 mL, powder) | | |
| Grated lemon zest | 1 tsp. | 5 mL |
| Dried oregano | 1/2 tsp. | 2 mL |
| Salt | 1/2 tsp. | 2 mL |
| Pepper | 1/4 tsp. | 1 mL |
| Lean ground lamb | 1 lb. | 454 g |
| Mayonnaise | 1/3 cup | 75 mL |
| Chili sauce | 2 tbsp. | 30 mL |
| Hamburger buns, split | 6 | 6 |

Preheat broiler. Combine first 9 ingredients in large bowl.

Add lamb. Mix well. Divide into 6 equal portions. Shape into 4 to 5 inch (10 to 12.5 cm) diameter patties. Arrange on greased broiler pan. Broil on top rack in oven for 4 to 5 minutes per side until no longer pink inside.

Combine mayonnaise and chili sauce in small cup. Spread on cut sides of bun halves. Serve patties in buns. Makes 6 burgers.

*1 burger: 423 Calories; 26.3 g Total Fat (11.4 g Mono, 4.4 g Poly, 8.7 g Sat); 59 mg Cholesterol; 28 g Carbohydrate; 1 g Fibre; 17 g Protein; 707 mg Sodium*

**BEEF BURGERS:** Use same amount of lean ground beef instead of lamb.

COACH

If you don't have a broiler pan, place a greased wire rack in a baking sheet with sides.

# Turbo-Charged Macaroni

*Bacon, tomato and chipotle pepper rev up this mac and cheese.*
*Serve with a green salad for a complete meal.*

| | | |
|---|---|---|
| Water | 12 cups | 3 L |
| Salt | 1 1/2 tsp. | 7 mL |
| Elbow macaroni | 3 cups | 750 mL |
| Bacon slices, diced | 8 | 8 |
| Garlic cloves, minced | 2 | 2 |
| (or 1/2 tsp., 2 mL, powder) | | |
| Can of tomato sauce | 25 oz. | 680 mL |
| Salsa | 1/2 cup | 125 mL |
| Finely chopped chipotle peppers in adobo sauce (see Coach, below) | 1 tsp. | 5 mL |
| Grated Mexican cheese blend | 2 cups | 500 mL |

Combine water and salt in Dutch oven. Bring to a boil. Add macaroni. Boil, uncovered, for 6 to 8 minutes, stirring occasionally, until tender but firm. Drain. Return to same pot. Cover to keep warm.

Meanwhile, cook bacon in large frying pan on medium for about 4 minutes until starting to brown. Add garlic. Heat and stir for about 1 minute until fragrant.

Add next 3 ingredients. Stir. Reduce heat to medium-low. Simmer, partially covered, for 10 minutes to blend flavours. Add macaroni. Stir.

Preheat broiler. Sprinkle cheese over macaroni mixture. Broil on centre rack in oven (see Coach, page 95) for 3 to 4 minutes until cheese is melted and golden. Makes about 6 1/2 cups (1.6 L).

*1 cup (250 mL): 481 Calories; 24.6 g Total Fat (9.0 g Mono, 2.7 g Poly, 14.7 g Sat); 49 mg Cholesterol; 47 g Carbohydrate; 3 g Fibre; 18 g Protein; 1173 mg Sodium*

Chipotle chili peppers are smoked jalapeño peppers. Be sure to wash your hands after handling. To store any leftover chipotle chili peppers, divide into recipe-friendly portions and freeze, with sauce, in airtight containers for up to one year.

# Rum Apple Pork

*The perfect example of gourmet fare in minutes! These crisp pork cutlets are simply delicious with dried apples in a sweet rum sauce.*

| | | |
|---|---|---|
| Large eggs | 2 | 2 |
| Fine dry bread crumbs | 2/3 cup | 150 mL |
| Paprika | 1 tsp. | 5 mL |
| Salt | 1/2 tsp. | 2 mL |
| Pepper | 1/4 tsp. | 1 mL |
| Cooking oil | 1 tbsp. | 15 mL |
| Pork cutlets (about 1 lb., 454 g) | 4 | 4 |
| Apple juice | 2/3 cup | 150 mL |
| Honey | 1/3 cup | 75 mL |
| Dark (navy) rum | 3 tbsp. | 50 mL |
| Brown sugar, packed | 2 tbsp. | 30 mL |
| Dijon mustard | 1 tbsp. | 15 mL |
| Soy sauce | 1 tbsp. | 15 mL |
| Dried apple | 1 cup | 250 mL |

Beat eggs with fork in large shallow dish.

Combine next 4 ingredients in small bowl. Transfer to large plate.

Heat cooking oil in large frying pan on medium. Dip pork into egg. Press both sides of pork into bread crumb mixture until coated. Add to frying pan. Cook for about 5 minutes per side until no longer pink inside. Transfer to plate. Cover to keep warm. Remove pan from heat. Wipe clean with paper towels.

Combine next 6 ingredients in small bowl. Add to same frying pan. Bring to a boil. Reduce heat to medium-low.

Add apple. Simmer for about 5 minutes until apple is plump. Pour over pork. Serves 4.

*1 serving:* 558 Calories; 15.7 g Total Fat (7.3 g Mono, 2.3 g Poly, 4.4 g Sat); 146 mg Cholesterol; 75 g Carbohydrate; 4 g Fibre; 23 g Protein; 1049 mg Sodium

# Ginger Mint Lamb Chops

*Lamb and mint are just meant to go together. This is an easy-to-make, elegant, restaurant-style entree of thick, tender lamb chops with a fresh-tasting, sweet-and-tangy mint drizzle.*

| | | |
|---|---|---|
| Lamb loin chops (about 2 lbs., 900 g) | 8 | 8 |
| Salt | 1/2 tsp. | 2 mL |
| Pepper | 1/4 tsp. | 1 mL |
| Fresh mint leaves, lightly packed | 1/2 cup | 125 mL |
| Fresh parsley leaves, lightly packed | 1/2 cup | 125 mL |
| Olive (or cooking) oil | 2 tbsp. | 30 mL |
| Lime (or orange) juice | 1 tbsp. | 15 mL |
| Liquid honey | 1 tbsp. | 15 mL |
| Ground ginger | 1 tsp. | 5 mL |
| Garlic powder | 1/2 tsp. | 2 mL |

Preheat broiler. Sprinkle lamb with salt and pepper. Arrange on greased wire rack set in foil-lined baking sheet with sides. Broil on centre rack in oven for about 6 minutes per side until desired doneness.

Meanwhile, put remaining 7 ingredients into blender. Process until smooth. Drizzle over lamb. Serves 4.

*1 serving: 517 Calories; 37.3 g Total Fat (17.7 g Mono, 2.9 g Poly, 13.9 g Sat); 131 mg Cholesterol; 10 g Carbohydrate; 2 g Fibre; 34 g Protein; 407 mg Sodium*

Lamb cooked at a medium doneness will reach an internal temperature of 150°F (65°C).

# Angel Delight Trifle

*The first great thing about trifle is that you've obviously handcrafted it with care. The second great thing about trifle is that you don't actually have to bake a thing. The third? The strawberry-soaked fluffy cake enveloped in creamy vanilla pudding.*

| | | |
|---|---|---|
| Torn angel food cake (bite-sized pieces) | 5 cups | 1.25 L |
| Container of frozen strawberries in light syrup, thawed | 15 oz. | 425 g |
| Box of instant vanilla pudding powder (4-serving size) | 1 | 1 |
| Milk | 1 1/2 cups | 375 mL |
| Frozen whipped topping, thawed | 2 cups | 500 mL |

Put cake into large glass bowl. Spoon strawberries with syrup over cake.

Beat pudding powder and milk in medium bowl for about 2 minutes until thickened. Spread evenly over strawberries.

Spread whipped topping evenly over top. Chill for 10 minutes. Serves 8.

*1 serving: 514 Calories; 5.0 g Total Fat (0.3 g Mono, 0.2 g Poly, 4.4 g Sat); 3 mg Cholesterol; 110 g Carbohydrate; trace Fibre; 11 g Protein; 950 mg Sodium*

# Berry Cake Cups

*Sponge cake topped with citrus cream and fresh berries is sure to draw plenty of oohs and aahs from the crowd. If berries are out of season, you can use thawed, frozen mixed berries.*

| | | |
|---|---|---|
| Block of cream cheese, softened | 8 oz. | 250 g |
| Icing (confectioner's) sugar | 1/2 cup | 125 mL |
| Lemon juice | 2 tbsp. | 30 mL |
| Grated lemon zest | 2 1/2 tsp. | 12 mL |
| Sponge cake berry cups | 6 | 6 |
| Fresh blueberries | 1 1/2 cups | 375 mL |
| Quartered fresh strawberries | 1 1/2 cups | 375 mL |

*(continued on next page)*

Sweets & Treats

Beat first 4 ingredients in medium bowl for about 3 minutes until smooth.

Place cake cups on 6 dessert plates. Spoon cream cheese mixture into cups.

Spoon blueberries and strawberries over cream cheese mixture. Makes 6 cake cups.

*1 cake cup: 292 Calories; 15.7 g Total Fat (3.8 g Mono, 0.6 g Poly, 8.8 g Sat); 61 mg Cholesterol; 34 g Carbohydrate; 2 g Fibre; 5 g Protein; 263 mg Sodium*

Pictured on page 89.

**Variation:** Combine blueberries and strawberries in small bowl before preparing cream cheese mixture. Add 2 tbsp. (30 mL) orange liqueur. Stir. Let stand until ready to spoon over cakes.

# Chocolate Nachos

*Here's your chance to get creative and turn convention on its head. Serve these crisp tortillas with cinnamon sugar and a chocolate drizzle at your next get-together and your guests will think you are oh so clever.*

| | | |
|---|---|---|
| Granulated sugar | 1/4 cup | 60 mL |
| Ground cinnamon | 2 tsp. | 10 mL |
| Ground ginger | 1/4 tsp. | 1 mL |
| Flour tortillas (9 inch, 22 cm, diameter) | 4 | 4 |
| Cooking oil | 2 tbsp. | 30 mL |
| Semi-sweet chocolate chips | 1/3 cup | 75 mL |
| Sour cream | 1/4 cup | 60 mL |

Preheat oven to 350°F (175°C). Combine first 3 ingredients in small bowl.

Brush tortillas with cooking oil. Sprinkle cinnamon mixture over top. Cut tortillas into 8 wedges each. Arrange wedges in single layer on 2 greased baking sheets with sides. Bake on separate racks in oven for about 10 minutes, switching position of baking sheets at halftime, until edges are golden.

Meanwhile, put chocolate chips into 1 cup (250 mL) liquid measure. Microwave, uncovered, on medium (50%) for 20 to 30 seconds at a time, stirring in between, until chocolate is almost melted. Do not overheat. Add sour cream. Stir until smooth. Spoon into small resealable freezer bag with tiny piece snipped off 1 corner. Drizzle chocolate in decorative pattern over wedges. Makes 32 wedges.

*1 wedge: 45 Calories; 2.4 g Total Fat (0.8 g Mono, 0.3 g Poly, 0.8 g Sat); 1 mg Cholesterol; 6 g Carbohydrate; trace Fibre; 1 g Protein; 40 mg Sodium*

# Chocolate Fudge Sauce

*Canned just can't compare. Use hot or cold.*
*Store in the fridge for up to two weeks.*

| | | |
|---|---|---|
| Butter (or hard margarine) | 1/2 cup | 125 mL |
| Granulated sugar | 1 cup | 250 mL |
| Cocoa, sifted if lumpy | 3/4 cup | 175 mL |
| Evaporated milk (or half-and-half cream) | 2/3 cup | 150 mL |
| Vanilla extract | 2 tsp. | 10 mL |

Melt butter in medium saucepan on medium.

Whisk sugar and cocoa into butter. Slowly add evaporated milk, stirring constantly with whisk, until smooth. Heat and stir for about 4 minutes until boiling. Remove from heat.

Add vanilla. Stir. Makes about 2 cups (500 mL).

*1/2 cup (125 mL): 467 Calories; 25.6 g Total Fat (6.8 g Mono, 1.0 g Poly, 16.1 g Sat); 63 mg Cholesterol; 61 g Carbohydrate; 4 g Fibre; 6 g Protein; 212 mg Sodium*

# Waffles Pseudo-Suzette

*No time to make crepes? Substitute frozen waffles and you have a sweet dessert (or extra-special brunch treat) with a delicious creamsicle taste.*

| ORANGE SAUCE | | |
|---|---|---|
| Butter (or hard margarine) | 1/2 cup | 125 mL |
| Granulated sugar | 1/4 cup | 60 mL |
| Orange juice | 1 cup | 250 mL |
| Grated orange zest | 2 tsp. | 10 mL |
| Orange liqueur (optional) | 1/4 cup | 60 mL |
| Blueberry (or plain) frozen waffles | 4 | 4 |
| Vanilla frozen yogurt | 2 cups | 500 mL |

**Orange Sauce:** Heat butter and sugar in small saucepan on medium-high, stirring occasionally, until butter is melted. Add next 3 ingredients. Stir. Bring to a boil. Reduce heat to medium. Cook for about 7 minutes, stirring occasionally, until mixture is slightly thickened. Makes about 1 cup (250 mL) sauce.

*(continued on next page)*

**138**

Meanwhile, toast waffles. Place waffles on 4 dessert plates. Spoon frozen yogurt over waffles. Spoon Orange Sauce over top. Serves 4.

*1 serving: 485 Calories; 29.9 g Total Fat (7.1 g Mono, 1.0 g Poly, 17.6 g Sat); 69 mg Cholesterol; 51 g Carbohydrate; 1 g Fibre; 6 g Protein; 410 mg Sodium*

# Pecan Raisin Tarts

*This traditional nut and raisin tart is the perfect dessert
to put out at holiday gatherings. Guaranteed to disappear quickly!*

| | | |
|---|---|---|
| Large egg | 1 | 1 |
| Brown sugar, packed | 1/2 cup | 125 mL |
| Coarsely chopped raisins | 1/4 cup | 60 mL |
| Corn syrup | 1/4 cup | 60 mL |
| Butter (or hard margarine), softened | 3 tbsp. | 50 mL |
| Finely chopped pecans | 2 tbsp. | 30 mL |
| Lemon juice | 1 1/2 tsp. | 7 mL |
| Vanilla extract | 1/2 tsp. | 2 mL |
| Salt | 1/8 tsp. | 0.5 mL |
| Unbaked tart shells | 12 | 12 |

Preheat oven to 375°F (190°C). Beat egg with fork in medium bowl until frothy. Add next 8 ingredients. Stir well.

Arrange tart shells on baking sheet with sides. Spoon raisin mixture into tart shells. Bake on bottom rack in oven for about 15 minutes until pastry is browned and filling rises to form a dome. Remove tarts from baking sheet and place on wire rack to cool. Makes 12 tarts.

*1 tart: 202 Calories; 10.4 g Total Fat (4.4 g Mono, 1.2 g Poly, 4.0 g Sat); 23 mg Cholesterol; 27 g Carbohydrate; 1 g Fibre; 2 g Protein; 187 mg Sodium*

Pictured on page 17.

You will find unbaked tart shells in the freezer section of your grocery store. For this recipe you'll need the 3 inch (7.5 cm) ones.

# Vanilla Rice Pudding

*This nostalgic fave with sweet, plump raisins and a hint of vanilla is sure to coax a sigh of contentment from your family and friends.*

| | | |
|---|---|---|
| Water | 1 cup | 250 mL |
| Raisins | 1/4 cup | 60 mL |
| Instant rice | 1 cup | 250 mL |
| Salt | 1/4 tsp. | 1 mL |
| Box of instant vanilla pudding powder (4-serving size) | 1 | 1 |
| Ground nutmeg | 1/8 tsp. | 0.5 mL |
| Milk | 2 cups | 500 mL |

Place medium plastic bowl in freezer. Combine water and raisins in medium saucepan. Bring to a boil. Add rice and salt. Stir. Remove from heat. Let stand, covered, for 5 minutes. Transfer to chilled bowl. Chill in freezer for 5 minutes.

Combine pudding powder and nutmeg in large bowl. Add milk. Beat for about 2 minutes until thickened. Add cooled rice mixture in 2 additions, stirring well after each addition. Chill in freezer for 10 minutes. Makes about 4 cups (1 L).

*1 cup (250 mL): 265 Calories; 1.5 g Total Fat (0.6 g Mono, 0.1 g Poly, 0.8 g Sat); 8 mg Cholesterol; 57 g Carbohydrate; 1 g Fibre; 7 g Protein; 582 mg Sodium*

# Quick Fruit Crumble

*Using canned fruit and filling makes quick work of this sweet crumble.*

| | | |
|---|---|---|
| Coarsely crushed vanilla wafers (about 25 wafers) | 1 cup | 250 mL |
| Plain spreadable cream cheese | 1/3 cup | 75 mL |
| Chopped pecans | 1/4 cup | 60 mL |
| Can of apple pie filling | 19 oz. | 540 mL |
| Can of sliced peaches in syrup, drained | 14 oz. | 398 mL |
| Ground ginger | 1/2 tsp. | 2 mL |
| Ground cinnamon | 1/4 tsp. | 1 mL |

Preheat oven to 400°F (205°C). Measure first 3 ingredients into medium bowl. Stir until mixture resembles coarse crumbs.

*(continued on next page)*

**140** Sweets & Treats

Combine remaining 4 ingredients in large bowl. Spoon into greased 2 quart (2 L) shallow baking dish. Sprinkle crumb mixture over top. Bake for about 15 minutes until bubbling and golden. Serves 4.

*1 serving: 434 Calories; 16.0 g Total Fat (6.0 g Mono, 1.9 g Poly, 5.5 g Sat); 25 mg Cholesterol; 74 g Carbohydrate; 5 g Fibre; 4 g Protein; 196 mg Sodium*

Pictured on page 143.

Don't confuse vanilla wafers with the popular ice cream wafers found with other sugary cookies. Vanilla wafers, although also found in the cookie aisle, come in a cardboard box and look like plain round cookies.

# Strawberries And Cream Sauce

*Guests will be delighted with this simply elegant fresh dessert.*

| | | |
|---|---|---|
| Cream cheese, softened | 4 oz. | 125 g |
| Granulated sugar | 2/3 cup | 150 mL |
| Milk | 1/2 cup | 125 mL |
| Vanilla extract | 1 1/2 tbsp. | 25 mL |
| Sliced fresh strawberries | 3 cups | 750 mL |

Beat cream cheese and sugar in small bowl until smooth.

Slowly add milk and vanilla, beating constantly, until sugar is dissolved.

Put strawberries into a medium bowl. Spoon cream cheese mixture over top. Makes about 4 cups (1 L).

*1 cup (250 mL): 291 Calories; 10.6 g Total Fat (3.0 g Mono, 0.6 g Poly, 6.4 g Sat); 33 mg Cholesterol; 45 g Carbohydrate; 2 g Fibre; 4 g Protein; 102 mg Sodium*

Always rinse your strawberries before hulling to avoid getting them waterlogged.

# Caramel Pineapple Sundaes

*Pining for pineapple? The flavours of caramel and tropical fruit combine*
*in this easy dessert option. Store extra sauce in an airtight container*
*in the fridge for up to two weeks. Microwave for 20 to 30 seconds to warm.*

### CARAMEL PINEAPPLE SAUCE

| | | |
|---|---|---|
| Brown sugar, packed | 1/2 cup | 125 mL |
| Butter (or hard margarine) | 3 tbsp. | 50 mL |
| Half-and-half cream | 1/3 cup | 75 mL |
| Can of pineapple tidbits, drained | 14 oz. | 398 mL |
| Vanilla ice cream | 2 cups | 500 mL |

**Caramel Pineapple Sauce:** Heat brown sugar and butter in small saucepan on medium for 4 to 5 minutes, stirring occasionally, until brown sugar is dissolved.

Add cream. Stir. Bring to a boil on medium. Boil gently for about 5 minutes, stirring occasionally, until mixture is thickened.

Add pineapple. Stir. Makes about 1 2/3 cups (400 mL) sauce.

Spoon ice cream into 4 dessert bowls. Spoon Caramel Pineapple Sauce over top. Makes 4 sundaes.

*1 sundae: 525 Calories; 28.9 g Total Fat (2.9 g Mono, 0.4 g Poly, 17.9 g Sat); 150 mg Cholesterol; 61 g Carbohydrate; 1 g Fibre; 6 g Protein; 158 mg Sodium*

**PINEAPPLE BANANA SPLITS:** Cut 4 bananas in half lengthwise. Place 1 half on each side of ice cream in dessert bowls. Add 1/4 cup (60 mL) sliced strawberries to each bowl. Pour sauce over top.

1. Quick Fruit Crumble, page 140
2. Lentil Feta Salad, page 50
3. Quick Pork Cassoulet, page 131

Props courtesy of: Casa Bugatti

# Double Chocolate Minis

*Get your chocolate fix, and double it for good measure, with these moist, chocolatey brownies bursting with chocolate chips.*

| | | |
|---|---|---|
| All-purpose flour | 3/4 cup | 175 mL |
| Cocoa, sifted if lumpy | 1/2 cup | 125 mL |
| Salt | 1/4 tsp. | 1 mL |
| Large eggs | 2 | 2 |
| Granulated sugar | 1 cup | 250 mL |
| Butter (or hard margarine), melted | 1/3 cup | 75 mL |
| Semi-sweet chocolate chips | 1 cup | 250 mL |

Preheat oven to 350°F (175°C). Combine first 3 ingredients in small bowl.

Whisk next 3 ingredients in medium bowl until combined. Add flour mixture. Stir well.

Add chocolate chips. Stir. Fill 24 greased and floured mini-muffin cups 3/4 full. Bake for about 15 minutes until wooden pick inserted in centre of brownie comes out moist but not wet with batter. Do not overbake. Makes 24 mini-brownies.

*1 mini-brownie: 129 Calories; 5.8 g Total Fat (0.9 g Mono, 0.2 g Poly, 3.5 g Sat); 22 mg Cholesterol; 18 g Carbohydrate; 1 g Fibre; 2 g Protein; 48 mg Sodium*

Pictured on page 144.

1. Tiramisu Parfaits, page 147
2. Double Chocolate Minis, above
3. Peach Strawberry Shortcakes, page 146

Props courtesy of: Winners Stores

# Peach Strawberry Shortcakes

*This traditional biscuit shortcake is tall on flavour and delightfully presented.*

| | | |
|---|---|---|
| Biscuit mix | 2 1/4 cups | 550 mL |
| Buttermilk (or soured milk, see Coach, page 42) | 1/2 cup | 125 mL |
| Butter (or hard margarine), melted | 1/4 cup | 60 mL |
| Granulated sugar | 1/4 cup | 60 mL |
| Sliced fresh strawberries | 3 cups | 750 mL |
| Can of sliced peaches in light syrup, drained and chopped | 14 oz. | 398 mL |
| Icing (confectioner's) sugar (optional) | 2 tbsp. | 30 mL |
| Frozen whipped topping, thawed | 3 cups | 750 mL |
| Slivered almonds, toasted (see Coach, page 63), optional | 1/4 cup | 60 mL |

Preheat oven to 400°F (205°C). Measure first 4 ingredients into large bowl. Stir until soft dough forms. Spoon into 6 mounds on greased baking sheet with sides. Bake for about 10 minutes until golden. Remove baking sheet to wire rack. Cool slightly.

Meanwhile, combine next 3 ingredients in small bowl.

Cut biscuits in half horizontally. Place bottom halves on 6 dessert plates. Top with 1/4 cup (60 mL) whipped topping. Spoon fruit mixture over top. Place top halves of biscuits over fruit mixture. Spoon remaining whipped topping over top.

Sprinkle with almonds. Makes 6 shortcakes.

*1 shortcake: 688 Calories; 34.6 g Total Fat (10.6 g Mono, 2.5 g Poly, 17.5 g Sat); 22 mg Cholesterol; 88 g Carbohydrate; 5 g Fibre; 11 g Protein; 1055 mg Sodium*

Pictured on page 144.

# Tiramisu Parfaits

*This is tiramisu without the fuss. The Tuscan truffle, as it is sometimes called, is an irresistible confection of creamy, smooth chocolate and coffee flavours.*

| | | |
|---|---|---|
| Cold strong prepared coffee | 3/4 cup | 175 mL |
| Rum extract | 1 tsp. | 5 mL |
| Vanilla extract | 1 tsp. | 5 mL |
| Tub of light cream cheese | 8 oz. | 250 g |
| Vanilla yogurt | 1 cup | 250 mL |
| Coarsely crushed vanilla wafers (about 40 wafers) | 1 1/2 cups | 375 mL |
| Cocoa, sifted if lumpy | 2 tsp. | 10 mL |

Combine first 3 ingredients in small cup. Set aside.

Beat cream cheese in small bowl until smooth. Add yogurt. Mix well.

To assemble, layer ingredients in 4 dessert bowls as follows:

1. 3 tbsp. (50 mL) wafer crumbs

2. 2 tbsp. (30 mL) coffee mixture

3. 1/4 cup (60 mL) cream cheese mixture

4. 2 tbsp. (30 mL) wafer crumbs

5. 1 tbsp. (15 mL) coffee mixture

6. 3 tbsp. (50 mL) cream cheese mixture

Sprinkle 1/2 tsp. (2 mL) cocoa over each parfait. Makes 4 parfaits.

*1 parfait: 526 Calories; 32.3 g Total Fat (12.3 g Mono, 2.2 g Poly, 16.0 g Sat); 66 mg Cholesterol; 49 g Carbohydrate; 1 g Fibre; 10 g Protein; 392 mg Sodium*

Pictured on page 144.

# Maple Apple Muffins

*These pretty muffins are full of apple, maple and cinnamon. Best served warm.*

| | | |
|---|---|---|
| All-purpose flour | 2 1/4 cups | 550 mL |
| Baking powder | 1 tbsp. | 15 mL |
| Ground cinnamon | 1 1/2 tsp. | 7 mL |
| Salt | 1 tsp. | 5 mL |
| Large eggs | 3 | 3 |
| Brown sugar, packed | 1 cup | 250 mL |
| Applesauce | 3/4 cup | 175 mL |
| Cooking oil | 1/3 cup | 75 mL |
| Maple (or maple-flavoured) syrup | 1/3 cup | 75 mL |
| Maple (or maple-flavoured) syrup | 2 tbsp. | 30 mL |

Preheat oven to 375°F (190°C). Measure first 4 ingredients into medium bowl. Stir. Make a well in centre.

Whisk next 5 ingredients in small bowl until combined. Add to well. Stir until just moistened. Fill 12 greased muffin cups 3/4 full. Bake for 18 to 20 minutes until wooden pick inserted in centre of muffin comes out clean.

Brush with second amount of syrup. Let stand in pan for 5 minutes. Remove muffins from pan and place on wire rack to cool. Makes 12 muffins.

*1 muffin: 261 Calories; 7.4 g Total Fat (4.1 g Mono, 2.0 g Poly, 0.8 g Sat); 47 mg Cholesterol; 46 g Carbohydrate; 1 g Fibre; 4 g Protein; 284 mg Sodium*

# Very Berry Melon Cooler

*A refreshing drink—and a perfect way to use up any leftover watermelon.*

| | | |
|---|---|---|
| Chopped watermelon | 2 cups | 500 mL |
| Frozen whole strawberries | 2 cups | 500 mL |
| Ginger ale | 1/3 cup | 75 mL |
| Lemon juice | 3 tbsp. | 50 mL |
| Granulated sugar | 2 tbsp. | 30 mL |
| Ice cubes | 6 | 6 |

*(continued on next page)*

Put first 5 ingredients into blender. Process until smooth.

Add ice cubes, one at a time, processing after each addition until smooth. Makes about 3 1/2 cups (875 mL).

*1 cup (250 mL): 174 Calories; 0.2 g Total Fat (trace Mono, 0.1 g Poly, trace Sat); 0 mg Cholesterol; 48 g Carbohydrate; 3 g Fibre; 1 g Protein; 6 mg Sodium*

To keep leftover pieces of melon from drying up, cover any cut surfaces with plastic wrap, pressing it tightly against the flesh so no air can get in.

# Dried Fruit Dips

*The newest chocolate-dipped darlings are all dried up. This treat is very unique.*

| | | |
|---|---|---|
| **Milk chocolate melting wafers** | **3/4 cup** | **175 mL** |
| **Dried apricots, mango, papaya and pineapple, cut into 2-bite pieces** | **8 oz.** | **225 g** |

Place chocolate wafers in small microwave-safe bowl. Microwave, uncovered, on medium (50%) for 1 minute. Stir. Microwave, uncovered, on medium (50%) for 20 to 30 seconds at a time, stirring in between, until chocolate is almost melted. Do not overheat. Stir until smooth.

Dip fruit pieces about halfway into chocolate. Place on waxed paper for about 10 minutes until set. Makes about 32 pieces.

*1 piece: 48 Calories; 1.5 g Total Fat (0 g Mono, 0 g Poly, 1.0 g Sat); 0 mg Cholesterol; 9 g Carbohydrate; 1 g Fibre; 1 g Protein; 4 mg Sodium*

**Variation:** Use white or dark chocolate melting wafers instead.

If your chocolate has become too thick for dipping, microwave for five seconds on medium. Stir.

# Measurement Tables

Throughout this book measurements are given in Conventional and Metric measure. To compensate for differences between the two measurements due to rounding, a full metric measure is not always used. The cup used is the standard 8 fluid ounce. Temperature is given in degrees Fahrenheit and Celsius. Baking pan measurements are in inches and centimetres as well as quarts and litres. An exact metric conversion is given below as well as the working equivalent (Metric Standard Measure).

## Spoons

| Conventional Measure | Metric Exact Conversion Millilitre (mL) | Metric Standard Measure Millilitre (mL) |
|---|---|---|
| 1/8 teaspoon (tsp.) | 0.6 mL | 0.5 mL |
| 1/4 teaspoon (tsp.) | 1.2 mL | 1 mL |
| 1/2 teaspoon (tsp.) | 2.4 mL | 2 mL |
| 1 teaspoon (tsp.) | 4.7 mL | 5 mL |
| 2 teaspoons (tsp.) | 9.4 mL | 10 mL |
| 1 tablespoon (tbsp.) | 14.2 mL | 15 mL |

## Cups

| Conventional Measure | Metric Exact Conversion Millilitre (mL) | Metric Standard Measure Millilitre (mL) |
|---|---|---|
| 1/4 cup (4 tbsp.) | 56.8 mL | 60 mL |
| 1/3 cup (5 1/3 tbsp.) | 75.6 mL | 75 mL |
| 1/2 cup (8 tbsp.) | 113.7 mL | 125 mL |
| 2/3 cup (10 2/3 tbsp.) | 151.2 mL | 150 mL |
| 3/4 cup (12 tbsp.) | 170.5 mL | 175 mL |
| 1 cup (16 tbsp.) | 227.3 mL | 250 mL |
| 4 1/2 cups | 1022.9 mL | 1000 mL (1 L) |

## Oven Temperatures

| Fahrenheit (°F) | Celsius (°C) |
|---|---|
| 175° | 80° |
| 200° | 95° |
| 225° | 110° |
| 250° | 120° |
| 275° | 140° |
| 300° | 150° |
| 325° | 160° |
| 350° | 175° |
| 375° | 190° |
| 400° | 205° |
| 425° | 220° |
| 450° | 230° |
| 475° | 240° |
| 500° | 260° |

## Dry Measurements

| Conventional Measure Ounces (oz.) | Metric Exact Conversion Grams (g) | Metric Standard Measure Grams (g) |
|---|---|---|
| 1 oz. | 28.3 g | 28 g |
| 2 oz. | 56.7 g | 57 g |
| 3 oz. | 85.0 g | 85 g |
| 4 oz. | 113.4 g | 125 g |
| 5 oz. | 141.7 g | 140 g |
| 6 oz. | 170.1 g | 170 g |
| 7 oz. | 198.4 g | 200 g |
| 8 oz. | 226.8 g | 250 g |
| 16 oz. | 453.6 g | 500 g |
| 32 oz. | 907.2 g | 1000 g (1 kg) |

## Pans

| Conventional Inches | Metric Centimetres |
|---|---|
| 8x8 inch | 20x20 cm |
| 9x9 inch | 22x22 cm |
| 9x13 inch | 22x33 cm |
| 10x15 inch | 25x38 cm |
| 11x17 inch | 28x43 cm |
| 8x2 inch round | 20x5 cm |
| 9x2 inch round | 22x5 cm |
| 10x4 1/2 inch tube | 25x11 cm |
| 8x4x3 inch loaf | 20x10x7.5 cm |
| 9x5x3 inch loaf | 22x12.5x7.5 cm |

## Casseroles

| CANADA & BRITAIN Standard Size Casserole | Exact Metric Measure | UNITED STATES Standard Size Casserole | Exact Metric Measure |
|---|---|---|---|
| 1 qt. (5 cups) | 1.13 L | 1 qt. (4 cups) | 900 mL |
| 1 1/2 qts. (7 1/2 cups) | 1.69 L | 1 1/2 qts. (6 cups) | 1.35 L |
| 2 qts. (10 cups) | 2.25 L | 2 qts. (8 cups) | 1.8 L |
| 2 1/2 qts. (12 1/2 cups) | 2.81 L | 2 1/2 qts. (10 cups) | 2.25 L |
| 3 qts. (15 cups) | 3.38 L | 3 qts. (12 cups) | 2.7 L |
| 4 qts. (20 cups) | 4.5 L | 4 qts. (16 cups) | 3.6 L |
| 5 qts. (25 cups) | 5.63 L | 5 qts. (20 cups) | 4.5 L |

# Coach Index

## A

Asparagus, trimming . . . . . . . . . 61

## B

Bacon, freezing . . . . . . . . . . . . . 69
Bananas, overripe, freezing . . . . . 39
Basil, fresh, using . . . . . . . . . . . . 83
Broiler pan, substitution . . . . . . . 132
Butter, substitution . . . . . . . . . . 121

## C

Chicken breast, quick cooking . . 103
Chicken breasts, cooking . . . . . . . 31
Chicken cuts, substitution . . . . . . 97
Chocolate, microwaving . . . . . . 149
Coconut, toasting . . . . . . . . . . . 63

## D

Dillweed, cooking . . . . . . . . . . . 65

## E

Eggs, hard-cooking . . . . . . . . . . 48
Eggs, poaching . . . . . . . . . . . . . 41

## F

Frying pans, using in oven . . . . . . 95

## G

Garlic, reducing odor . . . . . . . . 122
Gingerroot, peeling . . . . . . . . . . 58

## L

Lamb, assessing doneness . . . . . 135
Lemon, zesting . . . . . . . . . . . . . 80

## M

Meat thermometers . . . . . . . . . . 87
Meatball appetizers, serving . . . . . 25
Melon, storing . . . . . . . . . . . . . 149
Milk, soured, making . . . . . . . . . 42
Muffins, mixing . . . . . . . . . . . . . 28
Mushrooms, washing . . . . . . . . . 22

## N

Nuts, toasting . . . . . . . . . . . . . . 63

## P

Parsley, freezing . . . . . . . . . . . . 118
Peppers, chipotle, handling . . . . 133
Peppers, chipotle, storing . . . . . 133
Peppers, hot, handling . . . . . . . . 75
Peppers, hot, reducing heat . . . . . 75
Peppers, roasted, purchasing . . . . 40
Pizza sauce leftovers, freezing . . . 29
Pork, assessing doneness . . . . . . 128

## R

Red cabbage, preserving colour . . . 67

## S

Salads, serving . . . . . . . . . . . . . 49
Sandwiches, cutting . . . . . . . . . 105

Seafood, cooking . . . . . . . . . . . 117
Seeds, toasting . . . . . . . . . . . . . 63
Soups, freezing . . . . . . . . . . . . . 57
Steak, assessing doneness . . . . . . 87
Stir-fry, preparing ingredients . . 130
Strawberries, preparing . . . . . . . 141
Sugar snap peas, trimming . . . . . 61

## T

Tart shells, purchasing . . . . . . . . 139
Toasting nuts and seeds . . . . . . . 63
Tomato paste, freezing . . . . . . . . 79

## V

Vanilla wafers, purchasing . . . . . 141

# Recipe Index

## A

Angel Delight Trifle . . . . . . . . .136
Appetizers
　Bacon Mushroom Dip . . . . . .24
　Baja Bean Dip . . . . . . . . . . . .26
　Beef-Stuffed Mushrooms . . . .22
　Brie Happy . . . . . . . . . . . . . . .21
　Chipotle Meatballs . . . . . . . .25
　Cucumber Hummus Rounds .20
　Fire-Spiced Hot Wings . . . . . .27
　Green Olive Tapenade . . . . . .20
　Ham And Cheese Spirals . . . .24
　Red Hot Chicken Bites . . . . . .26
　Shrimp Crostini . . . . . . . . . .19
　Tropical Shrimp Dip . . . . . . .16
　Tuna Bruschetta . . . . . . . . . .23
Apple Muffins, Maple . . . . . . .148
Apple Pork, Rum . . . . . . . . . .134
Artichoke Rotini Salad . . . . . . .45
Artichoke Salmon . . . . . . . . . .111
Asparagus, Sun-Dried Tomato . .60

## B

Baby Bok Choy, Sesame . . . . . .63
Bacon Garlic Green Beans . . . .69
Bacon Mushroom Dip . . . . . . .24
Bagels, Pepperoni Pizza . . . . .29
Baja Bean Dip . . . . . . . . . . . . .26
Baked French Toast . . . . . . . .43
Baked Potato Champ . . . . . . .65
Baking
　Blueberry Lemon Muffins . . .42
　Buttery Orange Scones . . . . .39
　Chili Biscuit Flower . . . . . . .75
　Double Chocolate Minis . . . .145
　Feta Polenta Muffins . . . . . . .74
　Lemon Pepper Muffins . . . . .80
　Maple Apple Muffins . . . . . . .148
　Orange Chipper Muffins . . . .28
　Peach Strawberry Shortcakes .146

Peachy Keen Crepe . . . . . . . .37
Pecan Raisin Tarts . . . . . . . . .139
Quick Fruit Crumble . . . . . . .140
Quick Quiche Squares . . . . . .40
Balsamic Pork Chops . . . . . . . .128
Banana Splits, Pineapple . . . . .142
Barbecue Spice, No-Salt . . . . . .76
Barbecued Steak, Your Best . . .87
Basic Beef Sukiyaki . . . . . . . . . .84
Basil Sauce, Tomato . . . . . . . . .82
Basil Stir-Fry, Thai-riffic . . . . . .93
Basil Vinaigrette, Honey . . . . . .83
Bean Dip, Baja . . . . . . . . . . . . .26
Bean Soup, White . . . . . . . . . .56
Beans, Bacon Garlic Green . . . .69
Beef
　Basic Beef Sukiyaki . . . . . . . .84
　Beef Burgers . . . . . . . . . . . . .132
　Beef-Stuffed Mushrooms . . . .22
　Cheesy Portobellos . . . . . . . .92
　Chipotle Meatballs . . . . . . . .25
　Feel Good Cheeseburger
　　Macaroni . . . . . . . . . . . . . . .85
　Lazy Lasagna . . . . . . . . . . . . .94
　Meatza Pizza . . . . . . . . . . . . .34
　Mega Meatball Sandwiches .88
　Pineapple Meatballs . . . . . . .86
　Steak Salads . . . . . . . . . . . . .44
　Stroganoff Noodles . . . . . . . .95
　Taco Salad . . . . . . . . . . . . . . .49
　Tater Surprise . . . . . . . . . . . .91
　Thai-rrific Basil Stir-Fry . . . . . .93
　Your Best Barbecued Steak . .87
Beef Burgers . . . . . . . . . . . . . . .132
Beef-Stuffed Mushrooms . . . . .22
Berry Cake Cups . . . . . . . . . . . .136
Berry Melon Cooler, Very . . . . .148
Beverages
　Protein Power Shake . . . . . . .29
　Tropical Burst . . . . . . . . . . . . .38
　Very Berry Melon Cooler . . . .148
Biscuit Flower, Chili . . . . . . . . .75

BLT Salad . . . . . . . . . . . . . . . . .47
Blueberry Lemon Muffins . . . . .42
Blueberry Maple Topping . . . .82
Bok Choy, Sesame Baby . . . . . .63
Braised Red Cabbage . . . . . . . .67
Bread, Italian Garlic . . . . . . . . .76
Breakfasts, Brunches & Lunches
　Baked French Toast . . . . . . . .43
　Blueberry Lemon Muffins . . .42
　Brunch Special . . . . . . . . . . . .30
　Buttery Orange Scones . . . . .39
　Curried Waldorf
　　Chicken Wraps . . . . . . . . . .31
　Denver Noodle Frittata . . . . .32
　Easy Eggs Benny . . . . . . . . . .41
　Fresh Breakfast Salad . . . . . . .38
　Maple Apple Muffins . . . . . . .148
　Meatza Pizza . . . . . . . . . . . . .34
　Orange Chipper Muffins . . . .28
　Peachy-Keen Crepe . . . . . . . .37
　Pepperoni Pizza Bagels . . . . .29
　Protein Power Shake . . . . . . .29
　Quick Quiche Squares . . . . . .40
　Tropical Burst . . . . . . . . . . . . .38
　Turkey Pita . . . . . . . . . . . . . . .33
　Turkey Wrap . . . . . . . . . . . . .33
Brie Happy . . . . . . . . . . . . . . . .21
Browned Butter Fettuccine . . . .121
Brunch Special . . . . . . . . . . . . .30
Bruschetta, Tuna . . . . . . . . . . .23
Burgers, Beef . . . . . . . . . . . . . .132
Burgers, Lamb . . . . . . . . . . . . .132
Butter Fettuccine, Browned . . .121
Butter Sauce, Lemon . . . . . . . .81
Buttery Orange Scones . . . . . .39

## C

Cabbage, Braised Red . . . . . . .67
Cajun Chicken Po' Boys . . . . . .105
Cake Cups, Berry . . . . . . . . . . .136
Caramel Pineapple Sauce . . . . .142

**152**

Caramel Pineapple Sundaes . . .142
Carrot Soup, Ginger . . . . . . . .58
Carrots, Glazed Dill . . . . . . . .64
Carrots, Snap-To-Attention
   Peas And . . . . . . . . . . . . . .61
Cassoulet, Quick Pork . . . . . . .131
Champ . . . . . . . . . . . . . . . . . .65
Champ, Baked Potato . . . . . . .65
Champ, Southwestern . . . . . . .65
Cheese Spirals, Ham And . . . . .24
Cheeseburger Macaroni,
   Feel Good . . . . . . . . . . . . . .85
Cheesy Portobellos . . . . . . . . .92
Chic Chicken Chili . . . . . . . . .106
Chi-Chi Chicken Fingers . . . . . .103
Chicken & Turkey
   Cajun Chicken Po' Boys . . . .105
   Chic Chicken Chili . . . . . . . .106
   Chi-Chi Chicken Fingers . . . .103
   Chicken Mole . . . . . . . . . . .101
   Chicken Picadillo . . . . . . . . .102
   Chicken Salad Fiesta . . . . . . .52
   Chicken Tofu Stir-Fry . . . . . . .100
   Crispy Chicken Cutlets . . . . .96
   Curried Waldorf
      Chicken Wraps . . . . . . . .31
   Easy Chicken Paprikash . . . . .104
   Easy Quesadillas . . . . . . . . . .98
   Fire-Spiced Hot Wings . . . . . .27
   First-Class Chicken Curry . . . .99
   Red Hot Chicken Bites . . . . . .26
   South Seas Chicken . . . . . . . .97
   Thai Chicken Salad . . . . . . . .46
   Turkey Pita . . . . . . . . . . . . . .33
   Turkey Wrap . . . . . . . . . . . . .33
Chicken Mole . . . . . . . . . . . . .101
Chicken Picadillo . . . . . . . . . . .102
Chicken Salad Fiesta . . . . . . . .52
Chicken Tofu Stir-Fry . . . . . . . .100
Chickpeas, Sesame Ginger . . . .68
Chili Biscuit Flower . . . . . . . . . .75
Chilis
   Chic Chicken Chili . . . . . . . .106
   Thoroughly Modern Chili . . .116
   Vegetable Chili Pot . . . . . . .124

Chipotle Meatballs . . . . . . . . . .25
Chocolate Fudge Sauce . . . . . .138
Chocolate Minis, Double . . . . .145
Chocolate Nachos . . . . . . . . . .137
Chutney, Cucumber . . . . . . . . .73
Cioppino . . . . . . . . . . . . . . . .117
Clam Linguine, Garlic . . . . . . . .114
Cooler, Very Berry Melon . . . . .148
Couscous, Lemon Cranberry . .68
Couscous, Sweet Potato . . . . . .66
Cranberry Couscous, Lemon . .68
Cream Sauce, Strawberries And .141
Creamy Horseradish Sauce . . .81
Crepe, Peachy-Keen . . . . . . . . .37
Crispy Chicken Cutlets . . . . . . .96
Crostini, Shrimp . . . . . . . . . . . .19
Croutons, Garlic . . . . . . . . . . . .78
Crumble, Quick Fruit . . . . . . . .140
Cucumber Chutney . . . . . . . . .73
Cucumber Hummus Rounds . .20
Curried Waldorf Chicken Wraps .31
Curry, First-Class Chicken . . . . .99
Curry Their Favour Rice . . . . . .64
Cutlets, Crispy Chicken . . . . . .96

**D**

Denver Noodle Frittata . . . . . .32
Desserts
   Angel Delight Trifle . . . . . . .136
   Berry Cake Cups . . . . . . . . . .136
   Caramel Pineapple Sauce . . .142
   Caramel Pineapple Sundaes .142
   Chocolate Fudge Sauce . . . . .138
   Chocolate Nachos . . . . . . . . .137
   Double Chocolate Minis . . . .145
   Dried Fruit Dips . . . . . . . . . .149
   Maple Apple Muffins . . . . . . .148
   Orange Sauce . . . . . . . . . . . .138
   Peach Strawberry Shortcakes 146
   Pecan Raisin Tarts . . . . . . . . .139
   Pineapple Banana Splits . . . .142
   Quick Fruit Crumble . . . . . . .140
   Strawberries And
      Cream Sauce . . . . . . . . . . .141

Tiramisu Parfaits . . . . . . . . . .147
Vanilla Rice Pudding . . . . . . .140
Very Berry Melon Cooler . . . .148
Waffles Pseudo-Suzette . . . . .138
Dill Carrots, Glazed . . . . . . . .64
Dill Pickle Potato Salad . . . . . .48
Dill-icious Poached Salmon . . .110
Dill-icious Spring Soup . . . . . .57
Dips
   Bacon Mushroom . . . . . . . .24
   Baja Bean . . . . . . . . . . . . . .26
   Tropical Shrimp . . . . . . . . . .16
Double Chocolate Minis . . . . .145
Dressings & Vinaigrettes
   Honey Basil Vinaigrette . . . . .83
   Hot-And-Sour Dressing . . . . .50
   Pesto Vinaigrette . . . . . . . . .51
   Simple Dressing . . . . . . . . . .55
   Thai Dressing . . . . . . . . . . . .46
Dried Fruit Dips . . . . . . . . . . .149

**E**

Easy Chicken Paprikash . . . . . .104
Easy Eggs Benny . . . . . . . . . . . .41
Easy Quesadillas . . . . . . . . . . .98
Eggs Benny, Easy . . . . . . . . . . .41

**F**

Feel Good Cheeseburger
   Macaroni . . . . . . . . . . . . . . .85
Feta Polenta Muffins . . . . . . . .74
Feta Salad, Lentil . . . . . . . . . . .50
Fettuccine, Browned Butter . . .121
Fire-Spiced Hot Wings . . . . . . .27
First-Class Chicken Curry . . . . .99
Fish & Seafood
   Artichoke Salmon . . . . . . . . .111
   Cioppino . . . . . . . . . . . . . . .117
   Dill-icious Poached Salmon . .110
   Fish Tacos . . . . . . . . . . . . . .115
   Garlic Clam Linguine . . . . . . .114
   Honey Garlic Salmon . . . . . . .109
   Rum Runner Shrimp . . . . . . .113

**153**

Seafood Tagine . . . . . . . . . .112
Shrimp Crostini . . . . . . . . . .19
Thoroughly Modern Chili . . .116
Tropical Shrimp Dip . . . . . . .16
Tuna Bruschetta . . . . . . . . . .23
Fish Tacos . . . . . . . . . . . . . . .115
Florentine Mushrooms . . . . . .120
French Toast, Baked . . . . . . . .43
Fresh Breakfast Salad . . . . . . .38
Frittata, Denver Noodle . . . . . .32
Fruit Crumble, Quick . . . . . . .140
Fruit Dips, Dried . . . . . . . . . . .149
Fudge Sauce, Chocolate . . . . .138

**G**

Garlic Bread, Italian . . . . . . . .76
Garlic Clam Linguine . . . . . . .114
Garlic Croutons . . . . . . . . . . .78
Garlic Green Beans, Bacon . . . .69
Garlic Salmon, Honey . . . . . .109
Gazpacho, Spicy . . . . . . . . . .59
Ginger Carrot Soup . . . . . . . .58
Ginger Chick Peas, Sesame . . .68
Ginger Mint Lamb Chops . . . .135
Glazed Dill Carrots . . . . . . . . .64
Go-Withs
  Blueberry Maple Topping . . .82
  Chili Biscuit Flower . . . . . . . .75
  Creamy Horseradish Sauce . .81
  Cucumber Chutney . . . . . . .73
  Feta Polenta Muffins . . . . . .74
  Garlic Croutons . . . . . . . . . .78
  Honey Basil Vinaigrette . . . .83
  Italian Garlic Bread . . . . . . .76
  Kickin' Shrimp Sauce . . . . . .83
  Lemon Butter Sauce . . . . . .81
  Lemon Pepper Muffins . . . .80
  No-Salt Barbecue Spice . . . .76
  Speedy Sassy Salsa . . . . . . .79
  Spiced Sweet Pecans . . . . . .77
  Tomato Basil Sauce . . . . . . .82
  Tortilla Pesto Flutes . . . . . . .77
Green Beans, Bacon Garlic . . . .69

Green Olive Tapenade . . . . . . .20

**H**

Half-Baked, Completely-
  Good Potatoes . . . . . . . .62
Ham And Cheese Spirals . . . . .24
Ham Steaks, Spiced Orange . . .127
Hoisin Pork Stir-Fry . . . . . . . . .130
Honey Basil Vinaigrette . . . . . .83
Honey Garlic Salmon . . . . . . .109
Honey Pecan Pasta . . . . . . . . .118
Horseradish Sauce, Creamy . . .81
Hot-And-Sour Dressing . . . . . .50
Hot-And-Sour Slaw . . . . . . . . .50
Hot Wings, Fire-Spiced . . . . . .27
Hummus Rounds, Cucumber . .20

**I**

Italian Garlic Bread . . . . . . . . .76

**K**

Kickin' Shrimp Sauce . . . . . . . .83

**L**

Lamb Burgers . . . . . . . . . . . . .132
Lamb Chops, Ginger Mint . . . .135
Lasagna, Lazy . . . . . . . . . . . . .94
Lazy Lasagna . . . . . . . . . . . . .94
Lemon Butter Sauce . . . . . . . .81
Lemon Cranberry Couscous . . .68
Lemon Muffins, Blueberry . . . .42
Lemon Pepper Muffins . . . . . .80
Lentil Feta Salad . . . . . . . . . . .50
Lentil Stew, Sweet Potato . . . . .119
Linguine, Garlic Clam . . . . . . .114

**M**

Macaroni, Feel Good
  Cheeseburger . . . . . . . . . . .85
Macaroni, Turbo-Charged . . . .133

Maple Apple Muffins . . . . . . .148
Maple Topping, Blueberry . . . .82
Meatball Sandwiches, Mega . .88
Meatballs, Chipotle . . . . . . . . .25
Meatballs, Pineapple . . . . . . . .86
Meatless
  Browned Butter Fettuccine . .121
  Florentine Mushrooms . . . . .120
  Honey Pecan Pasta . . . . . . .118
  Mediterranean Pizza . . . . . .123
  Sweet Potato Lentil Stew . . . .119
  Swift Veggie Stir-Fry . . . . . .122
  Tofu Sukiyaki . . . . . . . . . . . .84
  Vegetable Chili Pot . . . . . . . .124
Meatza Pizza . . . . . . . . . . . . . .34
Mediterranean Pizza . . . . . . . .123
Mega Meatball Sandwiches . . .88
Melon Cooler, Very Berry . . . . .148
Mint Lamb Chops, Ginger . . . .135
Mole, Chicken . . . . . . . . . . .101
Muffins, see Baking
Mushroom Dip, Bacon . . . . . . .24
Mushrooms, Beef-Stuffed . . . . .22
Mushrooms, Florentine . . . . . .120

**N**

Nachos, Chocolate . . . . . . . . . .137
Noodles, see Pasta & Noodles
No-Salt Barbecue Spice . . . . . .76

**O**

Olive Tapenade, Green . . . . . .20
Orange Chipper Muffins . . . . .28
Orange Ham Steaks, Spiced . . .127
Orange Pork Stir-Fry . . . . . . . .129
Orange Sauce . . . . . . . . . . . .138
Orange Scones, Buttery . . . . . .39
Orange Teriyaki Stir-Fry . . . . . .70

**P**

Paprikash, Easy Chicken . . . . . .104
Parfaits, Tiramisu . . . . . . . . . .147

Pasta & Noodles
Artichoke Rotini Salad . . . . . .45
Browned Butter Fettuccine . .121
Denver Noodle Frittata . . . . .32
Feel Good Cheeseburger
    Macaroni . . . . . . . . . . . . .85
Garlic Clam Linguine . . . . . . .114
Honey Pecan Pasta . . . . . . .118
Lazy Lasagna . . . . . . . . . . . .94
Stroganoff Noodles . . . . . . .95
Thai Chicken Salad . . . . . . .46
Turbo-Charged Macaroni . . .133
Peach Strawberry Shortcakes . .146
Peachy-Keen Crepe . . . . . . . .37
Peas And Carrots,
    Snap-To-Attention . . . . . . . .61
Pecan Pasta, Honey . . . . . . . .118
Pecan Raisin Tarts . . . . . . . . . .139
Pecans, Spiced Sweet . . . . . . .77
Pepper Muffins, Lemon . . . . .80
Pepperoni Pizza Bagels . . . . . .29
Pesto Flutes, Tortilla . . . . . . . .77
Pesto Salad, Spinach . . . . . . .51
Pesto Vinaigrette . . . . . . . . . .51
Picadillo, Chicken . . . . . . . . . .102
Pickle Potato Salad, Dill . . . . . .48
Pineapple Banana Splits . . . . . .142
Pineapple Meatballs . . . . . . . .86
Pineapple Sauce, Caramel . . . .142
Pineapple Sundaes, Caramel . .142
Pita, Turkey . . . . . . . . . . . . . . .33
Pizza Bagels, Pepperoni . . . . .29
Pizza, Meatza . . . . . . . . . . . . .34
Pizza, Mediterranean . . . . . . .123
Po' Boys, Cajun Chicken . . . . .105
Poached Salmon, Dill-icious . . .110
Polenta Muffins, Feta . . . . . . .74
Pork
    Bacon Mushroom Dip . . . . . .24
    Bacon Garlic Green Beans . . .69
    Balsamic Pork Chops . . . . . . .128
    BLT Salad . . . . . . . . . . . . . . .47

Brunch Special . . . . . . . . . . .30
Denver Noodle Frittata . . . . .32
Easy Eggs Benny . . . . . . . . . .41
Ham And Cheese Spirals . . . .24
Hoisin Pork Stir-Fry . . . . . . .130
Meatza Pizza . . . . . . . . . . . . .34
Orange Pork Stir-Fry . . . . . . .129
Pepperoni Pizza Bagels . . .29
Quick Pork Cassoulet . . . . . .131
Rum Apple Pork . . . . . . . . . .134
Spiced Orange Ham Steaks . .127
Turbo-Charged Macaroni . . .133
Portobellos, Cheesy . . . . . . . .92
Potatoes
    Baked Potato Champ . . . . . .65
    Champ . . . . . . . . . . . . . . . .65
    Dill Pickle Potato Salad . . . .48
    Half-Baked, Completely-Good
        Potatoes . . . . . . . . . . . . .62
    Southwestern Champ . . . . .65
    Spicy Potato Wedges . . . . . .60
    Tater Surprise . . . . . . . . . . . .91
Protein Power Shake . . . . . . .29
Pudding, Vanilla Rice . . . . . . .140

Q

Quesadillas, Easy . . . . . . . . . .98
Quiche Squares, Quick . . . . . .40
Quick Fruit Crumble . . . . . . . .140
Quick Pork Cassoulet . . . . . . .131
Quick Quiche Squares . . . . . .40
Quick Tomato Soup . . . . . . . .59

R

Raisin Tarts, Pecan . . . . . . . . .139
Red Cabbage, Braised . . . . . .67
Red Hot Chicken Bites . . . . . .26
Rice, Curry Their Favour . . . . .64
Rice Pudding, Vanilla . . . . . . .140
Rotini Salad, Artichoke . . . . . .45

Rum Apple Pork . . . . . . . . . . .134
Rum Runner Shrimp . . . . . . . .113

S

Salads
Artichoke Rotini Salad . . . . . .45
BLT Salad . . . . . . . . . . . . . . .47
Chicken Salad Fiesta . . . . . . .52
Dill Pickle Potato Salad . . . . .48
Fresh Breakfast Salad . . . . . . .38
Hot-And-Sour Slaw . . . . . . . .50
Lentil Feta Salad . . . . . . . . . .50
Simple Salad . . . . . . . . . . . . .55
Spinach Pesto Salad . . . . . . .51
Steak Salads . . . . . . . . . . . . . .44
Taco Salad . . . . . . . . . . . . . . .49
Thai Chicken Salad . . . . . . . .46
Salmon, Artichoke . . . . . . . . . .111
Salmon, Dill-icious Poached . . .110
Salmon, Honey Garlic . . . . . . .109
Salsa, Speedy Sassy . . . . . . . .79
Sandwiches, Mega Meatball . .88
Sauces
    Blueberry Maple Topping . . .82
    Caramel Pineapple Sauce . . .142
    Chocolate Fudge Sauce . . . . .138
    Creamy Horseradish Sauce . .81
    Cucumber Chutney . . . . . . . .73
    Kickin' Shrimp Sauce . . . . . . .83
    Lemon Butter Sauce . . . . . . .81
    Orange Sauce . . . . . . . . . . . .138
    Speedy Sassy Salsa . . . . . . . .79
    Tomato Basil Sauce . . . . . . . .82
Scones, Buttery Orange . . . . . .39
Seafood, see Fish & Seafood
Seafood Tagine . . . . . . . . . . . .112
Sesame Baby Bok Choy . . . . . .63
Sesame Ginger Chickpeas . . . .68
Shake, Protein Power . . . . . . . .29
Shortcakes, Peach Strawberry . .146
Shrimp Crostini . . . . . . . . . . . .19

**155**

Shrimp Dip, Tropical . . . . . . . .16
Shrimp, Rum Runner . . . . . . .113
Shrimp Sauce, Kickin' . . . . . . .83
Sides
  Bacon Garlic Green Beans . . .69
  Baked Potato Champ . . . . . .65
  Braised Red Cabbage . . . . . .67
  Champ . . . . . . . . . . . . . . .65
  Curry Their Favour Rice . . . . .64
  Glazed Dill Carrots . . . . . . . .64
  Half-Baked, Completely-
    Good Potatoes . . . . . . . . .62
  Lemon Cranberry Couscous .68
  Orange Teriyaki Stir-Fry . . . . .70
  Sesame Baby Bok Choy . . . . .63
  Sesame Ginger Chickpeas . . .68
  Snap-To-Attention Peas
    And Carrots . . . . . . . . . . .61
  Southwestern Champ . . . . . .65
  Spicy Potato Wedges . . . . . . .60
  Sun-Dried Tomato Asparagus .60
  Sweet Potato Couscous . . . . .66
Simple Dressing . . . . . . . . . . .55
Simple Salad . . . . . . . . . . . . . .55
Slaw, Hot-And-Sour . . . . . . . .50
Snap-To-Attention Peas
  And Carrots . . . . . . . . . . . . .61
Soups
  Cioppino . . . . . . . . . . . . . .117
  Dill-icious Spring Soup . . . . .57
  Ginger Carrot Soup . . . . . . .58
  Quick Tomato Soup . . . . . .59
  Spicy Gazpacho . . . . . . . . . .59
  White Bean Soup . . . . . . . . .56
South Seas Chicken . . . . . . . .97
Southwestern Champ . . . . . . .65
Speedy Sassy Salsa . . . . . . . . .79
Spice, No-Salt Barbecue . . . . . .76
Spiced Orange Ham Steaks . . .127
Spiced Sweet Pecans . . . . . . .77
Spicy Gazpacho . . . . . . . . . . . .59
Spicy Potato Wedges . . . . . . . .60
Spinach Pesto Salad . . . . . . . .51
Steak Salads . . . . . . . . . . . . . .44

Steak, Your Best Barbecued . . .87
Stew, Sweet Potato Lentil . . . . .119
Stir-Fries
  Basic Beef Sukiyaki . . . . . . . .84
  Chicken Tofu Stir-Fry . . . . . .100
  Hoisin Pork Stir-Fry . . . . . . .130
  Orange Pork Stir-Fry . . . . . .129
  Orange Teriyaki Stir-Fry . . . . .70
  South Seas Chicken . . . . . . .97
  Swift Veggie Stir-Fry . . . . . .122
  Thai-rrific Basil Stir-Fry . . . . .93
  Tofu Sukiyaki . . . . . . . . . . . .84
Strawberries And Cream Sauce 141
Strawberry Shortcakes, Peach .146
Stroganoff Noodles . . . . . . . . .95
Stuffed Mushrooms, Beef- . . . .22
Sukiyaki, Basic Beef . . . . . . . . .84
Sukiyaki, Tofu . . . . . . . . . . . . .84
Sundaes, Caramel Pineapple . .142
Sun-Dried Tomato Asparagus .60
Sweet Potato Couscous . . . . .66
Sweet Potato Lentil Stew . . . . .119
Swift Veggie Stir-Fry . . . . . . . .122

## T

Taco Salad . . . . . . . . . . . . . . .49
Tacos, Fish . . . . . . . . . . . . . . .115
Tagine, Seafood . . . . . . . . . . .112
Tapenade, Green Olive . . . . . .20
Tarts, Pecan Raisin . . . . . . . . .139
Tater Surprise . . . . . . . . . . . . .91
Teriyaki Stir-Fry, Orange . . . . . .70
Thai Chicken Salad . . . . . . . . .46
Thai Dressing . . . . . . . . . . . . .46
Thai-rrific Basil Stir-Fry . . . . . .93
Thoroughly Modern Chili . . . .116
Tiramisu Parfaits . . . . . . . . . . .147
Tofu Stir-Fry, Chicken . . . . . . .100
Tofu Sukiyaki . . . . . . . . . . . . .84
Tomato Basil Sauce . . . . . . . .82
Tomato Soup, Quick . . . . . . .59
Topping, Maple Blueberry . . . .82
Tortilla Pesto Flutes . . . . . . . . .77

Trifle, Angel Delight . . . . . . . . .136
Tropical Burst . . . . . . . . . . . . .38
Tropical Shrimp Dip . . . . . . . . .16
Tuna Bruschetta . . . . . . . . . . .23
Turbo-Charged Macaroni . . . . .133
Turkey Pita . . . . . . . . . . . . . . .33
Turkey Wrap . . . . . . . . . . . . . .33

## V

Vanilla Rice Pudding . . . . . . . . .140
Vegetable Chili Pot . . . . . . . . . .124
Veggie Stir-Fry . . . . . . . . . . . . .122
Very Berry Melon Cooler . . . . .148
Vinaigrettes, see Dressings
  & Vinaigrettes

## W

Waffles Pseudo-Suzette . . . . . .138
Waldorf Chicken Wraps,
  Curried . . . . . . . . . . . . . . . .31
White Bean Soup . . . . . . . . . . .56
Wings, Fire-Spiced Hot . . . . . . .27
Wrap, Turkey . . . . . . . . . . . . . .33
Wraps, Curried Waldorf
  Chicken . . . . . . . . . . . . . . . .31

## Y

Your Best Barbecued Steak . . . .87

**156**

# Company's Coming cookbooks are available at retail locations throughout Canada!

EXCLUSIVE mail order offer on next page

Buy any 2 cookbooks—choose a 3rd FREE of equal or lesser value than the lowest price paid.

## Original Series — CA$15.99 Canada — US$12.99 USA & International

| CODE | | CODE | | CODE | |
|------|---|------|---|------|---|
| SQ | 150 Delicious Squares | CFK | Cook For Kids | WM | 30-Minute Weekday Meals |
| CA | Casseroles | SCH | Stews, Chilies & Chowders | SDL | School Days Lunches |
| MU | Muffins & More | FD | Fondues | PD | Potluck Dishes |
| SA | Salads | CCBE | The Beef Book | GBR | Ground Beef Recipes |
| AP | Appetizers | RC | The Rookie Cook | FRIR | 4-Ingredient Recipes |
| SS | Soups & Sandwiches | RHR | Rush-Hour Recipes | KHC | Kids' Healthy Cooking |
| CO | Cookies | SW | Sweet Cravings | MM | Mostly Muffins |
| PA | Pasta | YRG | Year-Round Grilling | SP | Soups |
| BA | Barbecues | GG | Garden Greens | SU | Simple Suppers |
| PR | Preserves | CHC | Chinese Cooking | CCDC | Diabetic Cooking |
| CH | Chicken, Etc. | PK | The Pork Book | CHN | Chicken Now |
| CT | Cooking For Two | RL | Recipes For Leftovers | KDS | Kids Do Snacks |
| SC | Slow Cooker Recipes | EB | The Egg Book | TMRC | 30-Minute Rookie Cook |
| SF | Stir-Fry | SDPP | School Days Party Pack | | |
| MAM | Make-Ahead Meals | HS | Herbs & Spices | | |
| PB | The Potato Book | BEV | The Beverage Book | | |
| CCLFC | Low-Fat Cooking | SCD | Slow Cooker Dinners | | |

## Cookbook Author Biography

| CODE | CA$15.99 Canada   US$12.99 USA & International |
|------|---|
| JP | Jean Paré: An Appetite for Life |

## Most Loved Recipe Collection

| CODE | CA$23.99 Canada   US$19.99 USA & International |
|------|---|
| MLA | Most Loved Appetizers |
| MLMC | Most Loved Main Courses |
| MLT | Most Loved Treats |
| MLBQ | Most Loved Barbecuing |
| MLCO | Most Loved Cookies |

| CODE | CA$24.99 Canada   US$19.99 USA & International |
|------|---|
| MLSD | Most Loved Salads & Dressings |
| MLCA | Most Loved Casseroles |
| MLSF | Most Loved Stir-Fries |
| MLHF | Most Loved Holiday Favourites |

**NEW** November 1/07

## 3-in-1 Cookbook Collection

| CODE | CA$29.99 Canada   US$24.99 USA & International |
|------|---|
| QEE | Quick & Easy Entertaining |
| MNT | Meals in No Time |

## Lifestyle Series

| CODE | CA$17.99 Canada   US$15.99 USA & International |
|------|---|
| DC | Diabetic Cooking |

| CODE | CA$19.99 Canada   US$15.99 USA & International |
|------|---|
| DDI | Diabetic Dinners |
| LCR | Low-Carb Recipes |
| HR | Easy Healthy Recipes |
| HH | Healthy in a Hurry |
| WGR | Whole Grain Recipes |

## Special Occasion Series

| CODE | CA$20.99 Canada   US$19.99 USA & International |
|------|---|
| GFK | Gifts from the Kitchen |

| CODE | CA$24.99 Canada   US$19.99 USA & International |
|------|---|
| BSS | Baking—Simple to Sensational |
| CGFK | Christmas Gifts from the Kitchen |
| TR | Timeless Recipes for All Occasions |

| CODE | CA$27.99 Canada   US$22.99 USA & International |
|------|---|
| CCEL | Christmas Celebrations |

| CODE | CA$29.99 Canada   US$24.99 USA & International |
|------|---|
| CATH | Cooking at Home **NEW** October 1/07 |

# Order **ONLINE** for fast delivery!

Log onto **www.companyscoming.com**, browse through our library of cookbooks, gift sets and newest releases and place your order using our fast and secure online order form.

| Title | Code | Quantity | Price | Total |
|-------|------|----------|-------|-------|
|  |  |  | $ | $ |
| DON'T FORGET to indicate your FREE BOOK(S). (see exclusive mail order offer above) please print |  |  |  |  |
|  |  |  |  |  |
|  |  |  |  |  |
|  |  |  |  |  |

**TOTAL BOOKS** (including FREE)

**TOTAL BOOKS PURCHASED:** $

|  | International | USA | Canada |
|--|---------------|-----|--------|
| **Shipping & Handling First Book** (per destination) | $ 11.98 (one book) | $ 6.98 (one book) | $ 5.98 (one book) |
| Additional Books (include FREE books) | $ ($4.99 each) | $ ($1.99 each) | $ ($1.99 each) |
| **Sub-Total** | $ | $ | $ |
| Canadian residents add GST/HST |  |  | $ |
| **TOTAL AMOUNT ENCLOSED** | $ | $ | $ |

## Terms
- All orders must be prepaid. Sorry, no CODs.
- Prices are listed in Canadian Funds for Canadian orders, or US funds for US & International orders.
- Prices are subject to change without prior notice.
- Canadian residents must pay GST/HST (no provincial tax required).
- No tax is required for orders outside Canada.
- Satisfaction is guaranteed or return within 30 days for a full refund.
- Make cheque or money order payable to: **Company's Coming Publishing Limited** 2311-96 Street, Edmonton, Alberta Canada T6N 1G3.
- Orders are shipped surface mail. For courier rates, visit our website: **www.companyscoming.com** or contact us: **Tel: 780-450-6223  Fax: 780-450-1857.**

## Gift Giving
- Let us help you with your gift giving!
- We will send cookbooks directly to the recipients of your choice if you give us their names and addresses.
- Please specify the titles you wish to send to each person.
- If you would like to include a personal note or card, we will be pleased to enclose it with your gift order.
- Company's Coming Cookbooks make excellent gifts: birthdays, bridal showers, Mother's Day, Father's Day, graduation or any occasion …collect them all!

☐ MasterCard   ☐ VISA   Expiry ____ / ____ MO/YR

Credit Card # _____

Name of cardholder _____

Cardholder signature _____

## Shipping Address  Send the cookbooks listed above to:
☐ **Please check if this is a Gift Order**

Name: _____

Street: _____

City: _____  Prov./State: _____

Postal Code/Zip: _____  Country: _____

Tel: (____) _____

E-mail address: _____
Your privacy is important to us. We will not share your e-mail address or personal information with any outside party.

☐ **YES! Please add me to your News Bite e-mail newsletter.**

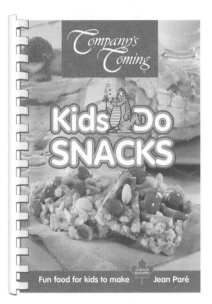

Know a budding chef who's eager to cook? Company's Coming presents *Kids Do Snacks*—a fun cookbook that lets kids become the masters of the kitchen. From *Blend It!* to *Bake It!,* the chapters are arranged so young cooks-in-training can learn more and more tricks and techniques as they go along—making it suitable for kids of all skill levels.

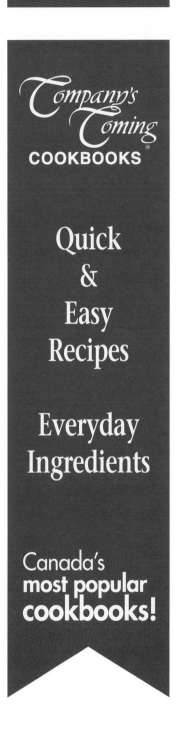

**Company's Coming COOKBOOKS®**

Quick & Easy Recipes

Everyday Ingredients

Canada's **most popular cookbooks!**